*Coleridge and Wordsworth
in Somerset*

By the same author:
A Somerset Journal
Quantock Country

COLERIDGE
AND
WORDSWORTH
IN SOMERSET

BERTA LAWRENCE

DAVID & CHARLES : NEWTON ABBOT

ISBN 0 7153 4944 9

Set in 11/13 pt Garamond
and printed in Great Britain by
Bristol Typesetting Co Ltd,
for David & Charles (Publishers) Limited
South Devon House Newton Abbot Devon
Distributed in the United States by Barnes & Noble

Contents

List of Illustrations

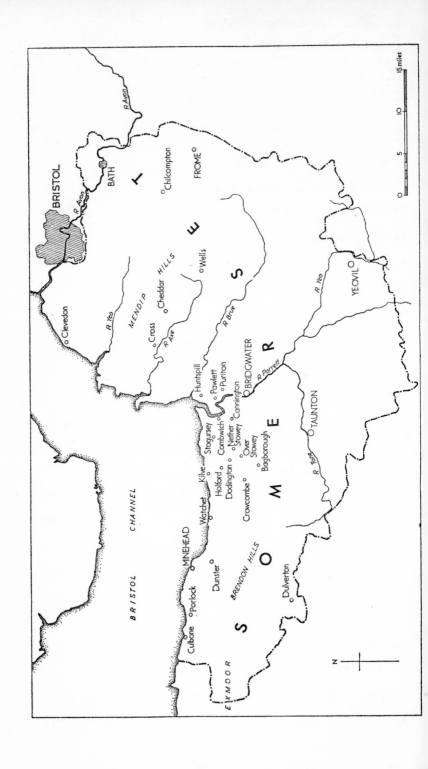

Introduction

This book aims at presenting a clear yet detailed picture of the period Coleridge and Wordsworth spent in Somerset. All the associations of the two poets with the Somerset places and people familiar to them have been drawn together in an attempt to make a plain and coherent pattern.

The book is not a work of literary criticism. Where Coleridge and Wordsworth are concerned, many critical and interpretive books have been written by some of the finest English and American scholars as well as a great number by non-academic writers. It must be stressed however, that the Somerset period was of major importance to Coleridge and Wordsworth as poets, particularly the year July 1797—July 1798 that they spent in proximity. For Wordsworth the period was formative and decisive, pointing him—and English poetry—to a new direction. For Coleridge it was the period of the full flowering of his poetic genius. Every one of Coleridge's greatest poems was written while he lived in Somerset and many of Wordsworth's greatest in the year immediately after his stay.

CHAPTER 1

NETHER STOWEY AND BRIDGWATER

If Coleridge had returned from the shades at any time between 1834, the year of his death, and 1968 he would have found Nether Stowey almost unchanged since his last visit in 1807. In spite of the housing-estates on the lower skirts of the Mount and alongside intersecting lanes, that until several years after World War II remained green-hedged and full of birds, he would have found the essential shape and structure of the place completely familiar: three streets forming a Y just as Collinson the traveller-historian noticed in 1791, with a brook from the Quantock Hills running down the longest. The main street, St Mary Street, stretches from the church to the George Inn and makes the supporting line of the Y. The two arms are Lime Street, where Coleridge's cottage stands at the western end, and Castle Street that climbs to the Mount, which is the gorse-grown and empty site of Nether Stowey castle.

However in 1968 the visitor's feet would have halted in uncertainty at a point about a quarter-mile distant from Stowey if he was approaching from the Bridgwater side, by way of the modern A39. Many a time Coleridge walked the eight miles from Bridgwater, sometimes after walking thirty-four from Bristol. Now, where the sight of the red sandstone tower of the church between the trees heralded his journey's end, part of the narrow winding road lies disused, the trees are thinner, and the new bypass has cut across green grassland to emerge from a field near the church where it incorporates a section of the old approach road (now considerably widened and with its curves straightened). It passes the church and the manor house called Stowey Court with its adjacent Stowey Court Farm and loops round the back of the village to emerge well outside it.

This bypass had been demanded by the inhabitants of Stowey for years. The increase of motoring, the popularity of Minehead during summer holidays, the many coach excursions to Porlock, Selworthy, Lynton, had choked the village with traffic and filled it with noise for several months of the year. Among the chief sufferers were the occupants of the little cottages in narrow Lime Street most of which were there in Coleridge's time and open directly on the street. Unfortunately the lovely group of church and manor house has now been cut off from the rest of the village so that church-goers and other pedestrians find their passage difficult and perilous, although the main part of the village has regained something of its former peace.

Farm, court-house, church; Coleridge's eyes would not find the group greatly changed, although a line of stables has become farm cottages and a cider-house put to other uses. The grey façade of the court-house, part of which was built by 1588, has hardly changed, and its long garden wall fronting the road, with a clipped yew hedge on its top, still bears, in spite of the shaking from roadworks machinery, the pretty eighteenth-century gazebo or summerhouse, with its Venetian window and ogee roof. When ladies sat there to look out during the period when Coleridge knew Stowey the traffic they saw was farm carts, the carrier's waggon, horse-chaises like Tom Poole's, the carriages of gentry like Mr Acland from Fairfield, Lord Egmont, the Luttrells at East Quantoxhead; but by the time Mrs Coleridge came back on visits, in 1823 with her young, attractive daughter and in 1830 by herself, lookers-out saw the coach for Minehead go rumbling by. Mrs Coleridge boarded it in Bridgwater, always very fussed beforehand, according to her letters, about whether she would find it crammed full when she stepped off the Regulator, the coach from Exeter.

A new graveyard has been made on the further side of the road. The old churchyard, approached by an avenue, contains an imposing memorial arch familiar to Coleridge; it commemorates members of the St Albyn family who were related to forefathers of the child Langley St Albyn, owner of Alfoxden when Wordsworth rented it. Close to the church door lies the slab tombstone commemorating Thomas Poole, the friend to whom Coleridge was incalculably indebted. The present Stowey blacksmith, a fine old craftsman, says that he was 'the last man to see Tom Poole's coffin' because, years ago, when the thrusting roots of a churchyard tree displaced it, he helped lift it out and replace it.

The church was largely rebuilt in 1851. It contains several things that Coleridge would recognise or whose sources he would remember although he never entered the church as a member of the congregation. A tablet on the south wall extols the splendid qualities of Tom Poole, and mentions his close friendship with Coleridge, Wordsworth and Southey. Another marble tablet commemorates Richard Jenkins Poole, Surgeon of Sherborne in the County of Dorset, who was Tom Poole's beloved younger brother Richard, and died in May 1798 at the age of twenty-nine. This brother was one of the very few Poole relatives who liked and admired Coleridge. Richard Poole wrote to him that he had read his poems 'with rapture' and ordered copies of *The Watchman*, Coleridge's unlucky periodical. He was liberal-minded and to some extent shared Coleridge's political views while deploring his passion in expressing them. His widow did not share this affection for Coleridge. She came to live in Stowey with her child and, as Coleridge said, showed great antagonism 'to me, my wife, even to my poor little boy', her rancour leading her 'into absolute insult' to Mrs Coleridge.

Another tablet at the west end of the church, on the north side of the tower arch, displays a grandiloquent Latin epitaph beneath the name Ricardo Camplin, Armiger, who died in 1792. Richard Camplin was agent for the Marquis of Buckingham, one of the greatest landowners in the neighbourhood (although he did not live there), and he carried out business transactions for the Stowey copper-mine which Coleridge mentioned in one of his letters from Germany. And the Latin epitaph was composed by Coleridge's friend William Bowles, a Wiltshire clergyman, and was the origin of six lines of poetry written at Stowey by Coleridge in 1797 of which the opening words are 'Depart in joy' and the title 'Translation of a Latin inscription by the Rev. W. L. Bowles in Nether Stowey Church'.

The roll of vicars' names on a wall shows that Dr William Langford took office in 1796. Like his predecessors he was frequently absent from Stowey but he was acquainted with Coleridge and, after both of them had left Stowey, wrote to Tom Poole that he would inquire among his friends with a view to arranging for Coleridge to act as travelling companion to any one of them leaving England for a warm climate, which Coleridge always insisted he needed.

The name of Dr Langford links with that of Coleridge in another, less direct way. When first appointed as vicar of Nether Stowey, he wished to make new arrangements about the church choir or the Stowey Singers as they were called. In connection with this, Tom Poole wrote to the absent Dr Langford in 1797, saying that if Dr Langford would send 'the Bassoon and the Music' that he had promised, the Singers would make good use of them. It would seem that the Stowey Singers included instrument-players in their number; there was certainly no organ in the church before 1886. There may, therefore, be grounds for the oft-repeated assertion that the 'loud Bassoon', mentioned in the 'Ancient Mariner' as providing the music at a wedding, owes its origin to this feature of Stowey church life, which Coleridge certainly heard discussed at Poole's.

Further up St Mary Street, and on the same side as Stowey Court, the modern vicarage stands in the grounds of the old vicarage (called the Old Rectory now) where the vicars of Stowey lived until about twenty years ago. Part of the older vicarage dates from 1680 although a considerable portion is Victorian. Not far beyond the vicarage gate one passes the carriage-entrance and the front door of The Old House, to which Tom Poole moved in about 1802, (see Chapter 2) which he altered and 'did-up', and where he entertained Coleridge in 1803 and 1807; Sara Coleridge and her children; and many of the most distinguished men of his time.

On the other side of St Mary Street and the brook there stands, neglected and forsaken, the fine eighteenth-century farmhouse of Stowey Farm whose finely proportioned rooms, some with oak panelling, one with ornamental plasterwork ceiling, undoubtedly resounded more than once with the 'eager musical energy' of Coleridge's talk, as Carlyle described it. Stowey Farm was rented by William Poole of Shurton to whose home Coleridge came in 1795 because Poole's grandson Henry was a college friend. William Poole's son, William also, may have lived in this farmhouse which now belongs to the Somerset County Council and has stood uninhabited for years.

In Coleridge's time Stowey did not possess an inn called the George although the present George Inn has existed for many years. The former George Inn had closed only a few years before the arrival of Coleridge and Wordsworth. It existed in 1789 when Walford the charcoal-burner, whose tragic story fascinated both of them, received a last drink of cider outside its doors as he passed in a cart on his way to execution. In the 1790s a Philip Hancock occupied premises referred to as 'the late George', and these premises were the present Oakford House situated near the brook, not far from the village centre.

The Rose and Crown Inn, on the opposite side of the street, was the property of Tom Poole and kept by Samuel Sully, an innkeeper for many years. No doubt it was pleasant and well-kept then, as it is now, since gentry did not scorn to dine there at special gatherings and the members of Poole's Female Benefit Society took tea there. But a seventeenth-century traveller left a written report of its flea-ridden squalor and of his sufferings when he spent a night there.

The three Stowey streets meet near the Victorian clock-tower at a point always called the Cross. Here, nowadays, Coleridge would miss a feature of Nether Stowey that lingered in a ramshackle state till after the mid-nineteenth century: the timber-framed, octagonal market-cross with its tiled roof, surmounted by a wooden turret supporting a clock and a bell that rang 'for divine service'. Later a new clock was substituted which, so tradition insists, Humphry Davy presented. In 1809 Coleridge enclosed in a letter written to Poole four sombre lines of verse entitled 'For a Market-Clock' or, in his notebook version 'Inscription proposed on a Clock in a market-place'. There is however no definite indication that he meant the inscription for the Stowey clock. The stocks stood close up to the market-cross.

When Coleridge walked the streets of Nether Stowey the place was a small market-town where he saw women from the farms of various villages clustering under the market-cross to sell their eggs and butter every Tuesday, which was market day. Horses drank from troughs near the market-cross. On Tuesday the blacksmith was specially busy, and at the time of Stowey fair, 18 September, even busier. So of course, were the two inns, the Rose and Crown and the Globe next to Tom Poole's house in Castle Street. The Globe Inn functioned until a few years ago when its premises became the house now called Globe House and retaining the old sign. This was the inn that figured in the Coleridge-Wordsworth 'spy' investigations as the government agent lodged there and talked to the landlord, Edward Tucker.

Most of the Castle Street houses on the right-hand side were there in Coleridge's time; so were the little brown and cream cottages lined up behind the brook. The large house called Castle Hill House, that now has bungalows built on part of its ground and others pressing close, belonged to a Mrs Pollard. Mrs Coleridge's letters imply that she knew her. South Lane, turning left higher up, leads on to Blindwell Lane and is a way Coleridge often used when walking to Bridgwater. Blind Well itself, a former holy well of which the water supposedly cured eye-diseases, is enclosed inside a garden.

Poole House, as Thomas Poole's house is called, has the most impressive façade in Castle Street, brick-built with a cornice, sash windows and other features of eighteenth-century buildings. The front door was moved in 1888 to the present central position from its original place, plainly visible today, near the left-hand side wall; it was at this time that the house became the premises of a corn chandler who left a wealth of corn-grains in the bedrooms for years afterwards. Before 1888 a tanner called Mr Hayman owned it, having bought it in 1845 from the trustees of Tom Poole's properties. Early in the twentieth century it became a grocer's house and shop-premises, and in recent years the shop portion has been a hairdresser's, a cake-shop, and a dress-shop for young children; its large plate-glass window mars the eighteenth-century front. Behind this window is Poole's 'great windy parlour' where Coleridge said he felt more at home than in his

Page 17 (left) The market cross in Nether Stowey stood at the junction of Lime Street and Castle Street. It was demolished many years ago;

(right) Unitarian Chapel in Dampiet Street, Bridgwater. Coleridge preached here

Page 18 (left) The gazebo at Nether Stowey;

(right) Tom Poole's bark-house, Nether Stowey

cottage, a room 20ft long with lofty ceiling and cut-moulded cornice. This is the room where Coleridge sat talking, far into the night with Poole, sometimes with Poole and Tommy Ward, the youthful tanner's apprentice, with Wordsworth and John Cruickshank, with Dorothy Wordsworth often present, all of them in the summer of life and Coleridge the gayest of the company. Here they brought Charles Lamb and Hazlitt, Charles Burnett, Joseph Cottle of Bristol. Here the Wedgwood brothers came. In this parlour Dorothy Wordsworth drank tea with old Mrs Poole as did the sharp-tongued Charlotte Poole of Marshmills when she came to see 'Aunt Thomas' and found there, to her displeasure, 'a certain Mr Coldridge', as she called him.

A door, now sealed up, led from the original parlour to the big kitchen that Mrs Coleridge remembered in absence as a warm and homely place where kindly old Mrs Poole presided over 'good old nurse' and several servants. It has been refloored, but people remember the old red-brick floor where the feet of the Poole household had worn a hollow round the table. The huge nails and old hooks for hams and flitches of bacon can be seen in the ceiling beams, and the original brass hook for the oil lamp in the ceiling. A sharply-turning back staircase leads up from the kitchen to a landing, where the floor contains some of the elm boards of Poole's time, and up to the vast attics, 70ft long, that were divided into five rooms for Poole servants; the pegs for their clothes have not been removed.

Three of the bedrooms possess a little dressing-room each, about 8ft square, lit by a sash window. Coleridge once wrote to Poole for a nailed-down deal box of papers left behind in 'your little room'. The main staircase leads up from what is now a hall with a fireplace to a balustraded landing onto which opens the most interesting room in the house; a room that can also be approached from the garden behind the house by an outside flight of worn stone steps with a door at the top (now a glass-paned one). This was Tom Poole's first Book Room. Its beautifully made barrel ceiling has bent-elm rafters and its floor is made of old elm boards fixed with flat nails which may have been made by the blacksmith who made the iron hinges for the original door that opens on the landing.

B

To this room Coleridge escaped from the smallness and clutter of his cottage, hurrying down his garden to cut across the tanyard and Poole's garden before mounting the stone steps to sit talking with Poole by the fireside without fear of interruption from grand-motherly Mrs Poole or chattering Sara. Here he could browse among Poole's well-stocked shelves or read the volumes belonging to the Stowey Book Society, by the light of the oil lamp hung from the brass hook still fixed to the ceiling.

Behind the house, walls of rough red stone enclose a tiny cobbled courtyard, now being concreted, from which a door leads to Tom Poole's flagstoned cellar and under the courtyard there is a culvert with a trickle of water from the old mill-stream that in Coleridge's day ran past his cottage door, although today there are no signs of it near Coleridge Cottage—perhaps because of 'tapping'.

A visitor coming through the carriage-entrance can see signs of the sweep of Tom Poole's drive leading to his stables across the present garden that is bounded by a wall not present in Poole's time, as his tanyard lay behind the stables and stretched beyond the Globe Inn. The tanyard ground now belongs to several owners and cottages cover part of it so that the topography outlined in Coleridge's letters cannot easily be traced in detail. However ample vestiges of Poole's tanyard remain. The garden of Rose Cottage contains a filled-in tan-pit and a stone-floored building said to have been Tom Poole's office. Old red-brown sheds of Poole's stand not far from Poole's bark-house that is now used by a builder. It is a sturdy brown building with slatted shutters, oper-ated by levers of apple-wood, that controlled the circulation of air in its upper storey where Poole's men stacked and dried the strips of bark they had ripped from Quantock oaks.

'When your Ripping is over you will come' wrote Coleridge in February 1801 from Keswick. Here they ground the dried bark to powder in Poole's bark-mill in preparation for tanning the skins that lay steeping in the pits and that often sent their stink into Lime Street and Castle Street. In his garden, under the lime tree, Tom Poole constructed a rough rustic summer-house with slabs of oak-bark and trained a jessamine to grow over it—'the jasmine Harbour' he called it. Joseph Cottle feasted in this home-made arbour on bread and cheese washed down by Taunton ale in the company of Poole and Coleridge, all of them in the happiest of moods. The appearance of Coleridge's young wife with the baby Hartley in her arms—she had carried him down her own garden and across the tanyard—completed a perfect idyll, or so it seemed. Here Coleridge repeated some of his earliest poems to Tom Poole to whom he wrote, not long after, that when he shut his eyes he could conjure up the vision of Poole's arbour, an Elysium which he had often reached after passing 'Tartarean tan-pits' and Cerberus—a reference to one of Poole's dogs.

A little higher up Castle Street a lane called Tanyard Lane leads to the village school that Poole built in 1813. Its gable overhangs the former tanyard.

Older Stowey residents declare that they remember four great elm trees standing at the roadside outside Poole's house. William Hazlitt said that he sat 'drinking flip' under two fine elms at Poole's, in company with Coleridge, and Coleridge's poem 'Fears in Solitude' tells us that from the hill above Stowey his eyes discerned 'the four huge elms' that marked out his friend's house. Yet it is doubtful whether the same elms could have remained standing until perhaps, fifty years ago.

This house of Tom Poole's is No 65 on the Tithe map where the property is sketched as it was in 1840, three years after Poole's death.

The noisy brook tumbling from the Quantock Hills is one of the most pleasing features of Nether Stowey although it sends flood-water across the road into some of the houses at times of heavy rainfall. It was a feature specially dear to Coleridge and frequently recollected in absence. 'Dear Gutter of Stowy!' he once called it in a letter to Poole, adding with mock exaggeration that he would always love it better than any murmuring stream he might hear when lying in an Italian orange-grove. The term 'gutter' did not denote a place of filth although Tom Poole himself, by means of a sluice, sent waste stuff from his odorous tan-pits into the stream that flowed out under culverts into Castle Street. The word 'gutter' refers to the deeply-cut channel with brown-pebbled bed into which the stream discharges and along which it rushes downward to St Mary Street where its voice grows louder, and then towards the church where it flows under the road and across fields to the sea at Combwich. Coleridge saw it sometimes clear and shining with a trout or two in its waters, sometimes swollen and red-brown with Quantock topsoil, sometimes quietened and depleted by drought. This stream wells out of the side of Danesborough, highest but one of the Quantock Hills, and flows across the road, down Five Lords Combe, along a lane Dorothy Wordsworth often used when walking back to Holford, past the old yellow cottage where several generations of broomsquires have lived, down from the hamlet of Bincombe, which is part of Over Stowey, to make a loop right round the site of Nether Stowey's vanished castle. It worked the mill in Mill Lane, as well as others in Coleridge's time, and from Mill Lane, as mentioned, a lesser stream ran down from it to flow past his cottage door, making a light tinkle just audible through his bedroom window.

Lime trees in the back gardens of the cottages, most of which are as old as Coleridge's and crowd more closely to the pavement's edge, gave the name to Lime Street. We know that a shady lime in Tom Poole's garden provided the bower where Coleridge sat one summer day in 1797 writing his poem 'This Lime Tree Bower my Prison'. The cottage garden premises are locked up now; the lime trees have gone; the long pathway leading to Tom Poole's garden and to Cruickshank's house is covered with buildings; the well and its windlass that the Coleridges used for their drinking-supply remain, but are unused. The cottage at the western end of Lime Street, on the left as one leaves the village, is easily picked out by its plaque and a painted sign fixed where the sign of the former Coleridge Cottage Inn used to hang, but it is still an insignificant building in spite of the rather ugly addition tacked on to its western side and the newer block at the back. Tiles have replaced Coleridge's thatched roof and newer windows the low small-paned lattices, through one of which Wordsworth looked out on a spring day in 1798 and remarked in Hazlitt's hearing 'How beautifully the sun sets on that yellow bank!' It is not likely that the low wall, with its coping of blue lias and a little gate in the middle, stood in front of the cottage door when Coleridge occupied the house.

Somewhere in Lime Street there was a cottage for housing a few of the Nether Stowey poor. It was called the poorhouse and belonged to Tom Poole. Coleridge made a sarcastic reference to its inhabitants in a letter to his wife from Germany and to the horrible state of the primitive roadway in winter when cart-wheels and horses' hooves churned the mud to a morass. In modern times, before the construction of the bypass, cars, coaches and lorries shook the little cottages to their foundations. Some of these vehicles bring several thousands of people every year to visit the home Coleridge despised. Admission costs only 6d as there is little to see, only the parlour to the right of the lobby, with a blocked-up door opposite the window showing the old entrance to Sara Coleridge's kitchen. At one time, two low-ceilinged sloping-floored empty bedrooms were on view. The parlour holds little that could remind one of the living Coleridge yet this room was the shell that enclosed the first murmurings of much of his greatest poetry. On a moonlit, frosty night of February he looked out at the sparkling roofs of Lime Street and wrote his 'Frost at Midnight' while his fire burnt low and a film fluttered on the bars of the grate, betokening, as he reflected, the arrival of a stranger.

The village of Over Stowey was often called Upper Stowey at the time Coleridge knew it. Rather surprisingly its population numbered about 460 where that of Nether Stowey was only just under 600 although the place had town status. (The population of Nether Stowey at the last census numbered 689 and is at present calculated to be about 750.) Over Stowey is tiny and possesses a peaceful beauty that the years have not changed very much. Coleridge would find the core of the village perfectly familiar if he could come to it by one of his usual routes: he came by way of Castle Hill and Bincombe Green where he turned left; or by walking along South Lane and part of Blindwell Lane where he struck off up a right-hand lane to emerge near Crosse Farm at Over Stowey; or by walking to the end of Blindwell Lane to the hamlet of Marshmills. Today the road to the hills forks at Marshmills, but the right-hand division of the fork leading to Over Stowey church did not exist in Coleridge's time.

Coleridge would take the present left-hand division of the fork and go past the farm towards Adscombe, turning left before he reached Adscombe to emerge just below Over Stowey village school. At the head of the slope, next to the school and schoolhouse, stands the church with its Tudor bench-ends and eighteenth-century monuments to such long-abiding families as the Riches of Crosse Farm, and opposite the church is the Rectory and a line of old cottages. St Peter's Well, the former holy well where Coleridge stopped to look down into the water that mirrored the waving ferns growing around the well's mouth, lies in the yard of the low-roofed house with pink-washed walls that was the rectory in Coleridge's day and is now called the Old Rectory.

Tucked in a corner behind an ash tree there stands the grey Jacobean farmhouse of Crosse Farm which has a little gazebo perched on its garden wall. A number of farms with rich red ploughlands lie within Over Stowey boundaries, and their fields bear the vivid names noted down in the tax-lists of 1797: Cockley Land (Tom Poole's), Strawberry Hill, Fuzz Ground which is still furzy, Great Warren, Castle Ground, the site of an ancient fortification. The red deer that range the hills ravage their crops at times, as they did in the eighteenth century.

Over Stowey parish included several hamlets. There was Ely Green, now called Aley, consisting of six houses. There was Adscombe, whose four houses, including Adscombe Farm, lay beneath wooded slopes cut by combes always wet with streams and springs, and where Coleridge at one time ardently wished to live (See Chapter III, *The Adscombe Project*). As for Marshmills, which can be reached from the main A39 road by turning off it just past the tiny Cottage Inn at Keenthorne, that Coleridge must have known, its handful of houses and the accompanying mill were familiar to him from the days of first acquaintance with this part of Somerset. The pleasant house set at the corner where roads and lanes meet is Marsh Mill House (often just called Marshmills) that the Pooles built early in the eighteenth century. Recently repaired and cream-washed it faces a lovely garden and a fine view of the blue line of hills. Here Coleridge, with Southey, was brought in July 1794 when he was a twenty-two-year-old Cambridge student, lively, passionately revolutionary, passionately talkative, to meet the large Poole clan who disliked him—and he knew it—till the end of their lives, although he was always civilly received as Tom's friend.

By the middle of the nineteenth century this house was occupied

by Thomas Ward who had been Tom Poole's partner in the tanning business, and here he ran a little silk-mill. The Coleridges
always esteemed him highly. 'How is Mr Ward, that man of many
daughters?' Mrs Coleridge would inquire in her letters, years after
leaving Stowey. Ward's five spinster daughters were still living in
what the modern novelist Phyllis Bottome described as 'the Miss
Wards' gardened and espaliered mansion' in 1888 and were
curtsied-to as gentry. Mrs Henry Sandford, who was formerly
Margaret Elizabeth Poole and granddaughter of one of the Marshmills family, was at that same time writing her invaluable book
Tom Poole and his Friends for which some information about
Coleridge was gleaned from the recollections of the old Miss
Wards.

From Marshmills, Coleridge sometimes took the road to the
other Over Stowey hamlet called Plainsfield that boasted eight
houses and a mill. The present road, on one's left as one faces the
hills at Marshmills crossroads, did not exist. He took the road
past the Marshmills farm to the hamlet of Aley, and then followed
the old road over a hill through woods to Plainsfield where it
emerged near the mill. And it is certain that he came this way,
and the Wordsworths too, to follow the narrow lane and the
wayside stream where the yellow musk grows, to roam in
Cockercombe.

This lovely valley, with the equally beautiful Seven Wells
Combe and its continuation, Ramscombe, lies inside Over Stowey
boundaries. They lie between steeply curved hillsides and slope
down from the prehistoric trackway on the Quantock ridge which
they meet along the section bordered by gnarled beeches that is
known as the Drove Road and that looks towards Exmoor over
farmlands on the Taunton side of the Quantocks. (There is a dis-
tressing suggestion for putting a car-park here.) Ramscombe climbs
past Quantock Farm, Cockercombe runs out near the old wishing-
stone Triscombe Stone. The hillsides enclosing these combes have
been planted by the Forestry Commission with dark regiments of
conifers; hard roads have been laid for vehicles. The combes are
still places of beauty but must have been incomparably more
beautiful in the days when Coleridge and the Wordsworths walked
the red earth-tracks (which people who walked there before 1920

remember still) as they were then shaded by oaks, sycamores, silver birches, beeches and 'scores of brilliant rowans'. Even by Coleridge's time, however, the Quantock oaks had been so depleted by tanners and charcoal-burners that local tanners had to buy much of their timber elsewhere.

However, the roamer in the Quantocks still hears the running streams that delighted a poet's ear—as in 'Recollections of Love ' —and is able, like the Wordsworths, to plunge through forests of bracken and whortleberry, gorse and heather, to set his feet on little green sheep-paths or on slabs of rough stone trodden into the wet ground by shepherds or pedlars in days long gone. He still comes across reedy deer-ponds and rushy, boggy places black with peat. If lucky or knowledgeable, he may see fox, weasel, stoat, hare, a badger, the arrogant stag, a troop of graceful hinds, as Coleridge, Wordsworth and Dorothy must have done many a time, although wild flowers and songbirds are less abundant than in 1798.

Hill-sheep graze on the slopes; Coleridge and the Wordsworths came across them, half-hidden as they browsed among summer bracken, just as walkers do now and have done for centuries. Whether he owned a flock or just a few, any man from Nether Stowey, Over Stowey, Holford or from Crowcombe on the other side of the Quantocks, had rights of free pasture on parts of the hills, as he has now. Today, a number of ponies also run there and in the eighteenth century cows too were put on the hills. The Stowey and Holford sheep ranged hundreds of rough heathery acres called Stowey Customs. We know that Wordsworth was in contact with at least one poor cottager who owned a few sheep that grazed the Customs, and in Stowey there were many who kept sheep there and claimed the old rights of cutting firewood, furze for bread-ovens and ferns for the bedding of cattle. But all the agricultural workers, who made up just about half the male population of Stowey and Holford were extremely poor when Coleridge lived among them. Few earned more than 1s a day, 1s 4d for a long summer day's labour, with beer or cider. Women earned 6d, 8d in summer, also with cider. By 1797, however, men were trying to obtain contract labour which earned 4d a day more than day-labour. Shepherds got a wage of 8s.

Billingsley thought that the low prices of food in this part of Somerset counterbalanced the very low wages. Beef, veal, lamb were sold in Taunton at 4d a pound, a fowl for 2s, a goose 3s, but the beautifully written arithmetic-book of a schoolboy Simeon Poole sets down a bushel of wheat as costing 5s 4d, tea 3s 6d per pound, candles 4s 6d a dozen, sugar 13d per pound, worst of all a 4lb loaf cost 1s. As for fuel, Billingsley said that in 1797 wood got scarcer and dearer every year and that coal came from Wales, was of bad quality and high in price. (Coleridge owed a big bill for coals when he ran up some debts in Stowey.) It is obvious that when the agricultural workers made a hunger-march in 1801 in the Stowey district they had been hard-pressed for years. Men like Tom Poole tried to better the poor man's lot. But the Quaker Cornishman, William Jenkin, wrote: 'There are not a set of men that ever fell under my notice whose hardened-hearts are more the object of my detestation than the Somerset farmers . . . whose hearts are too callous to admit of the least sense of feeling for the sufferings of the starving poor around them'.

A sight Coleridge frequently saw on the farms in the Stowey neighbourhood, as well as on those in Taunton Deane, was the plough drawn by red oxen, yoked in pairs. In the steeper fields he saw horses used instead of carts, carrying sheaves on wooden crooks each side of the saddle and pots of manure slung each side of a pack-saddle.

There were certain places in the hills where Coleridge and Wordsworth saw men pursuing other tasks. Quarries where they dug sand or hewed out the red sandstone: disused quarries, over-hung by branches, must have constituted a hazard on Dorothy's midnight walks. Hollows and recesses set back in a hillside where the lime-burner had built his kiln. Lonely, beautiful places like Five Lords Combe where the charcoal-burner watched the slow burning of his oak-billets and left the print of his pits that are still visible. One charcoal-burner left signs of his occupation beside the present Quantock Trail in Seven Wells Combe. Coleridge and Wordsworth saw the lonely smoke-blackened men sitting by their 'domes' near which they slept for several nights on end, waking at intervals to tend the fire. Each solitary charcoal-burner built himself a rude hut of poles and grass-turves.

The 30-ft wooden post called Walford's Gibbet was a point on the Quantock landscape tragically associated with a charcoal-burner and one that for Coleridge and Wordsworth held intense interest and poignancy. Its site is marked on the Ordnance map. They reached it, as one does today, either by walking up Five Lords Combe from the lane to Holford that starts at Bincombe Green, or by turning off the main Minehead road to climb the winding Coach Road which still bears this old name that designated a road for wheeled traffic. The gibbet stood higher up, set back from the left-hand side of the then rough and stony road behind bracken, foxgloves, scrub-oak and beeches, in the shadow of Danesborough. Here, on a glorious summer morning in 1789, Tom Poole and a crowd of Stowey sightseers stood to witness the execution of the young charcoal-burner John Walford who, after sentence, had been conveyed there in a straw-filled cart. He loved an Over Stowey girl and a month after a forced marriage had murdered his half-witted wife in this place one Saturday night when she was on her way to drink at the Castle of Comfort Inn. Tom Poole told Coleridge and Wordsworth that John Walford asked to speak to the girl Ann Rice before he died, that she knelt in the straw and murmured a few words to him; that he said 'I am ready', that the crowd recited the Lord's Prayer, that after the death-moment the only sound in the hushed silence was the loud singing of birds in Danesborough oaks. It is well-known that Wordsworth's feelings were moved by this tragic tale and that at one time he started using it as material for a poem (see chapters on Wordsworth). But it remained in Coleridge's memory also. As long afterwards as 1809 he wrote in a letter to Tom Poole: 'But above all, if you have no particular objection . . . do, do let me have that divine narrative of Robert Walford which of itself, stamps you a Poet of the 1st class in the *pathetic* and the *painting* of poetry, so very rarely combined'. The editor of Coleridge's letters noted that on the manuscript of this letter Poole had corrected the name Robert to John.

Walford's cottage was situated somewhere in Bincombe, near the stream, probably in that same lane now marked 'Holford, Unfit for Motors' where a stream flows over the road near the broomsquire's cottage. No doubt Coleridge and the Wordsworths sometimes came across a broom-squire in the hills around Five Lords Combe where broom-squires cut birch-twigs and ash-poles until recent times.

Dorothy Wordsworth also wrote that they walked to the Miner's House. Did she mean the counting-house or one of the copper-miners' vanished cottages? In their frequent walks along the Minehead road past the Castle of Comfort Inn, she and Coleridge had only to look across the red ploughlands and well-watered pastures towards the tiny village of Dodington, all of which, except one holding, belonged to the Marquis of Buckingham, to see the red stone engine-house of the Stowey copper-mine. Mine-shafts extend under the Minehead road where the wagons, loaded with weighed ore and making for Bridgwater sometimes rumbled past Coleridge and Dorothy. Coleridge visited the copper-mine and in 1799 refused to visit the mines at Clausthal because he said he would see nothing new. The miners too were poor men and at times knew tragedy.

This was the milieu in which Coleridge had his home for about two years.

BRIDGWATER 1798

Coleridge knew Bridgwater well. He stayed there several times: at the home of his friend John Chubb; at the house of the Unitarian minister; and once, when walking to Cheddar, with the Wordsworths, at an inn that may have been the Bridgwater Arms in Fore Street—demolished a few years ago—where he once noted that all the linen was marked 'Stolen from the Bridgwater Arms'.

He had inevitably to pass through the town on his numerous walking journeys between Nether Stowey and Bristol. As a rule he either took a rest there when he had walked the thirty-five miles from Bristol, or waited at the Angel Inn for Tom Poole's chaise. On the rarer occasions when he took the coach from Bridgwater to Bristol he waited at the George Inn in George Lane (now George Street) and sometimes wrote a letter and drank tea while he waited. In the 1790s the George, the King's Head and the renowned Swan were the chief coaching-inns. The mail coach to

London set out every morning at 10 o'clock and the London—
Exeter coach passed through at four in the afternoon. The nearest
posting-stage to Bridgwater was the still-flourishing Piper's Inn
at Ashcott where in 1841 Wordsworth and his wife met their
daughter and new son-in-law for breakfast.

Coleridge's Bridgwater was a town of 3,500 inhabitants, about
an eighth of its present population. To see the place as it looked
in the last decade of the eighteenth century one must first strip
the town of Broadway, the dual carriage-way opened in 1964, and
of the new bridge that carries it over the river to link Taunton
Road with the open space called Penel Orlieu. Here traffic for
Minehead moves into North Street and out to the main Minehead
Road, or Quantock Road, as the section nearest Bridgwater is
generally known. This Quantock Road portion is another
twentieth-century road, part of the A39, and cuts through fields
that Coleridge knew. When walking between Bridgwater and
Nether Stowey Coleridge used the older Wembdon Road, the
present A3339, that turns right at the present Quantock Gateway
Hotel and leads to the village of Wembdon. This road joins the
main Minehead road again after climbing Wembdon Hill and
descending Sandford Hill, and when Coleridge walked it, it took
him past fields and orchards where houses stand today. The
Elizabethan Sandford Farm would, however, be a familiar landmark to him, and from there the road took him through the village
of Cannington and on to Nether Stowey.

Coming from Bristol Coleridge approached Bridgwater on its
eastern side. His road, the present A38, was a great turnpike road
noisy with carts, goods-waggons, carriages, men on horseback and
often with herds and flocks being driven to the famous Bridgwater
market. But the last few miles of his route, from the village of
Pawlett, were not that section of the present A38 running from
Pawlett to Bridgwater between factories, housing estates, new
churches, schools, shops. The two places were separated by wide
pastures, cornfields and orchards traversed by various paths and
tracks, one of which led across pastures to the river-crossing from
Pawlett to Combwich that he and the Wordsworths sometimes
used. Coleridge's road was the turning seen today opposite the
Shell Mex Depot at Dunball, on the present A38. He followed it

in the direction of Puriton, came down Puriton Hill and emerged at Crandon Bridge, near Knowle Hall, to join the modern A39, another turnpike road leading from Bridgwater to Bath and London. His road from Crandon Bridge into Bridgwater also ran between fields and orchards until he passed the ruined East Gate that stood near the present Broadway junction.

As he made his way through Eastover between shops, houses and various inns that included the White Hart, the Globe, the London, the Star, he saw ahead of him the masts and rigging of ships that crowded the river just below the bridge, ships of up to 300 tons burthen that plied to Spain, Portugal, the West Indies, Virginia, Newfoundland or carried various commodities from Bristol, slates from Cornwall, fleeces from Ireland, coals from Wales. At least twenty owners of coal vessels lived in Bridgwater, and thirty years later Mrs Coleridge travelled back to London on a coach with the talkative elderly widow of one of them who told her how the coal-boat had earned her large, fatherless family's livelihood. She was called Mrs Towells and lived in Friarn Street. Now that the flourishing woollen-cloth industry of Bridgwater had declined the port made the chief contribution to the town's prosperity and provided, in addition to abundant trade and £3,000 in customs-dues, work for ropemakers, sailmakers, boat-builders, whose premises were scattered in various streets and yards, as well as bountiful custom for the ships' chandlers and general merchants, whose shops stood along the Parret quaysides. The numerous quayside inns prospered—the Dolphin, the Anchor, the Fountain, the King's Arms, the Ship in Launch, and the riverside Salmon in Salmon Lane (now Salmon Parade).

Standing on the Town Bridge Coleridge watched the tidal river Parret flowing sullenly towards its estuary at Combwich (pronounced Cummidge). He wrote of it as 'the Parrot' and made the poor joke that it looked as filthy as if 'all the parrots in the House of Commons had been washing their consciences in it'. It would certainly be as muddy with red soil as it is now, and very dirty where it passed the quays, but as it did not contain the factory effluents and the sewage that contaminate it today, it was still clean enough for salmon to swim up as far as the bridge.

Sometimes when he looked down from the bridge he saw the

bore sweep up the river from the estuary, disturbing the ships at anchor and sometimes swamping barges as they carried coals or other goods up the Parret towards the river Tone and Taunton. The stone bridge, with its three arches and massive piers, was five centuries old when Coleridge came through Bridgwater on his early visits to Nether Stowey. Because its great piers dammed the tidal waters causing inconvenience to the boats, it was pulled down in 1795 and replaced by an iron one in 1797. For two years Coleridge, like everyone else, used a temporary wooden bridge supported on piles.

When he left the bridge he mingled with the carts and pedestrians in cobbled, narrow Fore Street where houses, shops and inns stood close together on each side, the shops representing a multitude of trades; staymakers, hatters, mercers, peruke-makers, maltsters, chandlers, tallow-chandlers, trunk-makers, china-and-earthenware dealers. In Fore Street alone the inns were numerous, including the Bridgwater Arms, the Ship and Castle, the King's Head. On the left-hand corner, past the bridge, Coleridge passed the Castle Inn with its stables, then the stone gateway of his friend John Chubb's very comfortable house, and, immediately next door, the squalid little gaol kept by William Briffett. Ahead of him he saw the tall spire of the noble parish church, St Mary's, piercing the air high above the half-timbered houses that stood on the market-place, now called the Cornhill. Behind these timbered houses and behind the shop-fronts of the south side of High Street, lay the two newly-built corn-and-provision markets. On market-days much of the bargaining went on in the open High Street in front of the busy Crown Inn sited where the Royal Clarence Hotel now stands. Frequently when returning from Bristol Coleridge walked to the back of the Crown to call at an inn situated behind it (the Clarence occupies both sites) that was called the Angel or often the Old Angel, the name Coleridge used. Letters, parcels, books were sometimes left for him at the Angel to be called for by himself, the Stowey carrier, or a messenger from Tom Poole.

When his own correspondence had to go by the expensive post instead of by a carrier's waggon, it was sent off, sometimes by Milton the unreliable carrier who brought them to Bridgwater, from the post office in a small shop next door to the Swan, one of the most famous coaching-inns in the west of England. (The Fine Fare supermarket stands close to its site.)

Coleridge probably came to Bridgwater just after the removal of the old Market Cross, sketched by his friend Chubb, which had left a convenient space for the hustings to be set up in the Cornhill. Whilst waiting for the Bristol coach one morning late in May 1796, Coleridge climbed onto the platform, paced about and cynically reflected on the bribe-taking and false promises that attended all elections. Bridgwater was a rotten borough, its Parliamentary elections steeped in corruption.

Both sides of the High Street right up to the market place were bordered with shops and a multitude of inns of which the Golden Ball, the Greyhound, the Lamb (now called the Duke of Monmouth), the Bull and Butcher, the Mansion House, still exist, although the Noah's Ark, the Woolpack and a good many others familiar to Coleridge's eyes have vanished. On the north side, the old Guildhall stood on the site of the present one; and next door, in place of today's Charter Hall, was the Assize Hall, where assizes were held in rotation with Wells and Taunton. Here John Walford was sentenced. Coleridge found John Chubb, a member of the corporation, too busy to see him, in Assize week.

A section of the High Street between the Mansion House Inn and the present Bristol Arms, was divided down the middle of the road by a narrow line of shops called the Island. They included the famous butchers' shops called the Shambles.

Penel Orlieu too boasted inns in plenty; the Blue Boar, still there, the Half Moon, the Valiant Soldier, now called the Market House, the Three Tuns on part of the Classic cinema site, and several more. They got enormous custom on Thursday, the principal market day, when fat cattle were sold in this place round the old market cross inelegantly called Pig Cross, that Coleridge passed on his way out through the ruined West Gate into North Street. He would see West Street with its colour-washed higgledy-piggledy cottages, stretching away to the Fair Field, where the great St Matthew's Fair had opened on St Matthew's Day since the days of King John. In September 1797 he saw West Street crammed with booths, stalls, penned sheep, cheapjacks, and with waggon-loads of Somerset people who came in from villages miles away for their big annual outing and spending-spree.

Coleridge certainly took De Quincey to see the ancient castle remains when they made a Sunday evening tour of the town, and if they walked past the remains of the North Gate they went close to the disused Glasshouse, an enormous beehive-shaped kiln used in manufacturing glass bottles, one of the landmarks most familiar to Coleridge. The medieval castle, destroyed in the Civil War, had occupied the present King Square where, in Coleridge's day, fine brick houses for prosperous burgesses were being built. He would show De Quincey all that remained of the castle in King Square; the Constable's House and a massive wall. Then, walking him down beautiful Castle Street—today still a delight to the eye with its two lines of early Georgian houses—he took him along the West Quay to look at the old Water Gate of the castle that still survives, as well as at the handsomest house in all the town, the large house called The Lions because of the stone lions guarding its steps that are flanked by stone balustrades and stone pavilions with Venetian windows. That prolonged Sunday evening tour of the town would include a walk through the churchyard to admire the church and a stroll along St Mary Street where several old houses they saw survive today, although the line of houses on the church-side has gone. The upper floor of the medieval priest's house (now the Steyning Tea Shop) was used by the boys of the free King James' Grammar School while some poor townspeople occupied the downstairs portion. A Baptist Meeting House stood where the present Baptist Church now stands. Judge Jeffreys' house (lodgings rather) now called Marycourt had not then lost its stone-mullioned windows. The building now called the Tudor Café existed, despite its present sham timbering, and the present inns The Rose and Crown, the Three Crowns, the Fleur de Lis, as well as several more. From Judge Jeffreys' House to the corner of Friarn Street extended the long wooden, tile-roofed structure of the Cheese Market that did tremendous trade and gave a name to the now-vanished inn called the Cheese House. Past the Fleur de Lis, near the place where St Mary Street ran into what is now Old Taunton Road, the South Gate stood in a state of fairly good preservation, as Chubb's sketch shows, not far from

Page 35 Medieval stone bridge over River Parret, Bridgwater, demolished between 1795 and 1797. John Chubb's warehouses and office are on the quayside. *(From a drawing by John Chubb)*

Page 36 South Gate, Bridgwater. Coleridge went through it when walking from Bridgwater to Taunton
(From a drawing by John Chubb)

the almshouse outside that disappeared in the nineteenth century. When Coleridge slept a night in Bridgwater before going on to Taunton he left by the South Gate.

Friarn Street on his right as he faced the way to Taunton, Dampiet Street on his left—how well he knew both these streets! And how familiar a sight to the householders was the raven-haired young man with the brilliant grey eyes, broad brow, and sensual mouth, who hurried past with an impetuous, almost zigzag walk —Hazlitt noticed that he could never walk straight—on his way to Dampiet Street to preach at the Unitarian church that everyone still called the Presbyterian Meeting House, or to visit John Howel the minister at the Parsonage House. The modern Broadway has swallowed up part of the old narrow Friarn Street and garages have replaced houses, yet much that Coleridge knew remains; the old Green Dragon, a few cottages, the large, handsome houses, backed by walled gardens, such as No 15 with its attractive shell-porch, and Ivy House where the Mayor, Robert Codrington, lived. The Quaker Meeting House in Friarn Street was then seventy years old, and the cottages to the left of its doorway stood there in Coleridge's day. On the right a paved courtyard gave room for the carriages of congregation members.

The Unitarian Meeting House in Dampiet Street had been largely rebuilt in 1790 but the new façade retained over its door the fine 'shell' that graced the original building of 1688 so admired by Defoe. This Meeting House is, in spite of the somewhat drab exterior, still one of the town's best buildings. When Coleridge knew it no other sect of Dissenters in the town possessed such a dignified place of worship.

Although Coleridge preached several times at the meeting house that is known as Christ Church Chapel, only two dates can be definitely stated: Sunday, 5 June 1797 when he had breakfasted in Taunton before the service, and Sunday, 7 January 1798 when he took duty for Mr Howel the minister who had taken his daughter to London for 'surgical assistance'. Among the well-kept records of Christ Church Chapel no mention can be found of Coleridge's visits and no private letter or journal is known that contains a contemporary reference to the impression he created. However he preached in Shrewsbury in that same month of

C

January, and we have the vivid, unforgettable account of him—his looks, his golden eloquence, his attack on war and the evils of the world, his praise of peace and purity of heart, his magnetic personality—written by William Hazlitt who, at the age of twenty, walked 'ten miles in the mud' from the home of his father, the Unitarian minister at Wem, to hear him. This was the same arresting poet-preacher who came to Bridgwater earlier in the month.

Mr Howel's friend, the Bristol Unitarian minister Mr Estlin, did observe in a letter that his preaching in Bridgwater met with considerable success. It seems impossible that the voice, language, sentiments of Coleridge could not have stirred in some degree those estimable and sober Somerset burgesses who sat below the canopied pulpit in the seats they rented at 5s a year. Foremost in the congregation were the trustees of the meeting house who shouldered all responsibilities, especially Thomas Osler, its treasurer and its sturdy pillar of support for sixty years as his marble tablet testifies. No doubt in accordance with Dissenters' usual practice, they all shook the visiting preacher's hand; Robert Osler, maltster; Thomas Osler, linen draper; Joseph Partridge, linen draper (who came from Taunton); Thomas Pyke, brazier (his bells, his brass chandeliers and dishes are found in many churches); William Dean, dealer in china who had a shop in the Island; Samuel Thomas, schoolmaster; Thomas Beaman, gentleman; William Osler, acomptant; and Thomas Cole, gentleman, an attorney-at-law who handled all business affairs of the chapel.

Members of the congregation combined to pay Mr Howel's meagre salary. Coleridge was desperately poor when he preached at the Meeting House that Sunday in January but no poorer than the minister. Mr Howel's salary, paid quarterly, never reached £50 per annum and in 1803 dropped to £43. (His successor worried a great deal about his salary.) During the vacant year 1805 Mr Cole, the attorney, received a letter from the Rev Joshua Toulmin who had accepted a ministry in Birmingham. Concerned that the Bridgwater congregation had no minister, and rather doubtful whether the income it could offer would be acceptable, he put forward the names of two Unitarian ministers who might be willing to fill the vacancy: Mr Jenkins of Whitchurch in Shrop-shire (whom Hazlitt mentions) and Mr Hazlitt of Wem in Shropshire, 'a man of superior intelligence who has seen much of the world'. This, of course, was young William Hazlitt's father.

Coleridge told Hazlitt, at the time of this visit, that he thor-oughly disapproved of infant baptism. His son Berkeley, born at Nether Stowey, was not baptised and neither was Hartley. If, as he once contemplated, he had ever applied to be assistant minister at Bridgwater, the baptism of children might have made a bone of contention for in 1798 John Howel baptised the infants Lewis Laurence, Samuel Badger and William Gwynne. A few years later Coleridge had all his children baptised together.

John Howel, who was buried under his vestry that is now the schoolroom, came to Bridgwater in 1793. Intended at first for the Anglican church he had turned to the Dissenting ministry for reasons of conscience, was educated at the Presbyterian College of Carmarthen, and served as minister at Enfield, Poole and at Yeovil where his acceptance of Unitarian principles drew criticism. During ten years at Bridgwater his gentle yet manly character won the love of his flock. He was a man of strong liberal sympathies, and it is significant that although Howel was too uninfluential to offer help, Coleridge appealed to him on behalf of his revolution-ary friend, Thelwall, before going to the well-off merchant John Chubb. Mr Howel enjoyed the free use of a house known as the Parsonage House, and in spite of the demolition that has taken place in its vicinity it has proved possible, though difficult, to establish its identity, although the Meeting House records show only that it was situated in Friarn Street on ground known as Sealys, that in 1833 part of its garden became the Unitarian burial ground, that the house ceased to be the Parsonage House in about 1850. A study of the Corporation Schedule of Property (1836) reveals that it was a double-fronted house standing on the north side of Friarn Street, in line with the Green Dragon Inn. Cal-culations based on this evidence point to the fact that the Parsonage House was the property now called the Old Armoury Garage which, in line with the Green Dragon and several pairs of old cottages, stands set back a little distance from the carriage-way. The bright blue paint on the doors and window-frames of its double-fronted house makes it conspicuous. A senior member of the Unitarian congregation recalls that the site of the petrol pumps was formerly a burial ground and that years ago she saw two old tombstones leaning against a wall of the house. (The name Old Armoury comes from the fact that the Territorials used to rent the building that is now the garage.)

A walk along narrow Green Dragon Lane gives a glimpse of a corner of the old Bridgwater that Coleridge saw when he came to the Parsonage House and stayed with the Howels for the night; the brickwork, the weathered tiles, the higgledy-piggledy arrangement of the buildings from the Green Dragon to the Old Armoury Garage reveal the age of the properties that are backed by walled gardens with ancient crooked trees.

It is almost certain that when Hazlitt was on his way home after his three-week visit to Stowey and Alfoxden he and Coleridge were put up for the night at the Parsonage House before starting the long walk to Bristol. Hazlitt carried home one regret, that he had not gone to hear Coleridge preach.

In Joshua Toulmin the Taunton minister, Coleridge recognised a remarkable man of greater intellectual force than the gentle, courteous John Howel. He was in his late fifties when Coleridge met him and the twenty-five year old Coleridge always spoke of him as 'the good old man'. Born in London, he was educated at St Paul's School and a Calvinist Academy, obtaining his earliest pastoral post as Presbyterian minister at Colyton, Devon, which he had to vacate when he turned to the Baptist persuasion. As his preaching talents were so striking the Unitarian Baptists at Taunton offered him the ministry of their church in Mary Street. Here he stayed for nearly forty years, preaching eloquent sermons, exerting himself to maintain a dwindling flock, writing numerous books, including his *History of Taunton* that Charles James Fox consulted and that has been re-edited, and professing liberal political views that in the 1790s brought persecution and suffering to all his family.

The large Toulmin family—he had twelve children—occupied a house in the east side of Fore Street with Mr John Bluet, the grocer, on one side and Dr Thomas Clitsom, the apothecary, on the other. To supplement the minister's low salary Mrs Toulmin kept a small bookshop and Mr Toulmin taught a few pupils. This house, where Coleridge came on several occasions, stood near the turning into Hammet Street on ground where modern shops have risen. In December the effigy of Tom Paine was burnt before its door and only the not-disinterested efforts of Dr Clitson and Mr Bluet saved the house itself. One evening a large stone hurled through the study window just missed Mr Toulmin's head. As he had already given up his school and the bookshop this renewed cruelty almost broke his spirit. His friends formed little bands of vigilantes to protect him, and his courage rallied. He staunchly refused 'calls' to other congregations, continued to uphold the rights of man in his public speaking and allowed little groups of 'democrats'—who even dared sing the Marseillaise—to meet at his house. In 1794 the University of Harvard conferred on him the diploma of Doctor of Divinity.

It may have been the period of persecution that unhinged the mind of the Toulmin daughter who drowned herself at Bere in Devon in 1798 when on Sunday, 13 May, Coleridge walked eleven miles to conduct the service in Dr Toulmin's place and recorded that the calamity had cut deep into Toulmin's heart.

In 1803 Dr Toulmin accepted the ministry of New Meeting, Birmingham, where he won great esteem and affection. When he died in 1815 many funeral sermons were preached in his honour, including one at Mary Street Chapel, Taunton. Several of Dr Toulmin's American descendants have visited the chapel; his son Harry became an American judge.

The chapel had been built in 1721 by a congregation that included wealthy burgesses as its elegant architecture testifies. The façade, remodelled in 1847, lacks the dignity of the interior. The pulpit where Coleridge preached is made of black oak richly carved in a design incorporating shells, vines, grapes, acanthus leaves, whose richness must have pleased Coleridge's eye as much as the graceful brass chandelier given in 1728, a rare specimen of Dutch workmanship.

It is not the chapel's only treasure. There are silver chalices old enough for them to have been displayed to Coleridge, and recently the wife of the present minister (of both Taunton and Bridgwater), the Rev E. Davies, discovered, under a load of coal-dust in a forgotten cupboard under the chapel stairs, two bells made of Nailsea glass, each with a loop at the top for a thong to pass through. Did Coleridge see these bells hung up in the chapel and struck with a padded hammer so that they gave out their soft clear ring to mark the period of silent prayer? Glass bells were used in this way in several meeting-houses.

Several books have been found marked on their flyleaf in Toulmin's hand 'Mary Street Chapel Library' followed by a number. These formed part of Toulmin's lending-library for the poor.

CHAPTER 2

THOMAS POOLE OF NETHER STOWEY

'Poole—my brother by gift of God'. S. T. Coleridge

He was born on 14 November 1765 at the house in Castle Street with the brook rushing past its door. His father Thomas Poole, who had brought his bride Elizabeth Buller there three years before, was son of a William Poole of Marshmills in Over Stowey. The family there included a son William who became a prosperous Stogursey farmer, a son Charles who settled in Taunton and whose perry and cider Tom Poole liked such guests as the Wedgwoods and Coleridge to drink; and a son John who became a tanner like Thomas and occupied the family house at Marshmills.

Coleridge said that his friend Tom Poole showed too intense an attachment for members of the Poole clan. He had in mind the Marshmills family who persistently disliked Coleridge. The father died in 1792 but three of his children knew Coleridge well: Charlotte, the acid-tongued girl whose diary shows powers of shrewd observation and a constant antipathy to Coleridge; John, a scholarly, conventional, stiff-necked Tory, who became Rector of Enmore and disliked Coleridge, Wordsworth and Southey to the end of his days; Penelope, dark-eyed and pretty, who married William Anstice and who in 1807 returned from her married home in Shropshire to visit her brother at Enmore rectory, visiting her old Enmore friend Mary Cruickshank as well. Coleridge wrote to Mary that he wished he had not missed seeing Penelope whom he admired and liked. Nevertheless, ten years earlier, Penelope had shared the family distaste for Tom's revolutionary friends. When Tom tactlessly brought the unwelcome Coleridge and

Wordsworth to Marshmills House one evening and asked his musical cousin Penelope to entertain them by singing Handel's 'Come, ever-smiling Liberty', she refused and sang another air, remarking later 'I knew what they meant by *their* liberty'.

Young Tom Poole fiercely envied his cousins and brother their education at Tiverton Grammar School and determined to educate himself, studying hard at night, reading Latin with his cousin John during John's vacation from Oxford and collecting books. He faced sneering discouragement from his irascible, gouty father, although he mastered every detail of their trade and insisted, two years before his father's death, on spending some months in Wantage, near Reading, as a common workman, wearing a tanner's working clothes. The legend grew up that during his stay he met Coleridge, then a trooper in the Dragoons in Reading.

From Purkis, the influential London tanner, he imbibed ideals of liberty, a hatred of despotism, a horror of war, a flaming desire for justice for the common man, a sense of responsibility towards the humble and inarticulate. Returning to Stowey he aired his novel views violently in all sorts of company, arguing hotly with the Over Stowey curate Mr Lewis at the Marshmills supper table and with cousin John when shooting woodcock on the Quantocks, insisting that 'if the French are conquered, Europe is enslaved'.

In the circumscribed world of Stowey and Bridgwater he became for richer people an object of intense suspicion, preacher of revolutionary doctrines, a public danger even. Hadn't he prevented the burning of Tom Paine's effigy in Stowey and lent a Stowey cabinet-maker Paine's book *The Rights of Man* which Symes the attorney very properly stamped on? Poole's Stowey Book Society was founded in 1793 but even the Rev John Poole, who co-operated, suggested after it came under suspicion that certain works were unsuitable for lending. The Men's Friendly Society, which Poole founded, was much more suspect and was mentioned by the government agent who reported on the Wordsworth 'Spy' affair. Feelings ran so high that Coleridge saw that he might endanger the society altogether if he persuaded Poole to assist his friend the republican Thelwall, admitting that Poole incurred 'great odium' for a time by installing Coleridge himself in Stowey.

Over the years Poole's integrity, his universal kindness, his prospering business, conquered local suspicion while a succession of visits from distinguished men made it plain that elsewhere he was held in high esteem. He became the friend of several local aristocrats such as the Earl of Egmont and Mr Acland of Fairfield, Stogursey. After his father's death in 1795 he inherited the tanning business as well as the Castle Street property, several Stowey houses and a number of fields that included Portray Meadow, Cockley Land, Nabhill and Currys Acre. When he withdrew from the business, apart from financial interest, he farmed nearly 200 acres, experimenting with breeds of sheep and methods of sowing wheat, although he despised the new threshing-machine used by William Cruickshank of Enmore.

He loved his workpeople; a lock of grey hair was found in his desk when he died, 'the hair of my poor shepherd who served me 23 years'. Coleridge reproached him with being wilfully blind to his servants' deceit and depravity. Mrs Coleridge, however, always wrote sentimentally of 'dear good old Nurse' and Martha, but was sarcastic about 'little consequential William', 'little conceited, shrewd-looking William', who, on later visits drove her in Poole's carriage to and from Bridgwater.

Like many bachelors Poole doted on his pets. When Coleridge lived at the cottage he kept the large dog which Coleridge nicknamed Cerberus; in later days Mrs Coleridge mentioned the poodle Carlo, and in later years the sagacious poodle Toby who carried a penny in a basket to the baker's every morning to buy a 'man-chip' for Poole's breakfast.

When Poole brought Coleridge to live in Stowey, he himself was just thirty, a solid and serious young man when compared with the ebullient Coleridge, and seemingly a settled-down bachelor. His mother kept house for him. She had a sweet nature, in spite of sufferings caused by 'the stone', and Poole loved her tenderly as did Coleridge and his wife. When she recovered from a severe illness Coleridge wrote Poole a letter containing affectionate messages for Mrs Poole, and wished her 'a long yellow sunset'.

After her death Poole travelled to France and Switzerland, even being presented to Bonaparte, then First Consul, another cause for scandal in Poole's native town. When visiting the Louvre, Poole saw Sir James Mackintock looking at a painting of an albatross, heard him repeat 'He shot the albatross', and stepped forward eagerly to tell him that his own dearest friend had written the poem about the mariner, written it in his own birthplace, Nether Stowey.

Two years later he found himself in London, employed by his friend the difficult but sterling John Rickman, secretary to the Speaker, on the difficult task of making an abstract of the thousands of replies returned by parish overseers after receiving government questionnaires about their relief of the poor. He worked for his expenses only, and for a while Coleridge and George Burnett shared his lodgings.

After Coleridge's departure to Malta in the spring of 1804, Poole returned to Nether Stowey, where he acquired almost unbounded affection. People made him executor of their estates, guardian of their children. The unemployed asked his aid, even an unemployed tanner from Hampshire, a desperate miner from Wales who had heard that the Stowey copper-mine might reopen. He opened a quarry on Castle Hill to provide a little work. His still-surviving Women's Benefit Society founded in 1806—his Men's Society has gone—was a boon to poorer women in old age, sickness and childbirth. Other places founded similar Women's Benefit Societies, and in his notebook Coleridge made a memorandum 'to speak to Lady Beaumont of Friendly Female Societies, Stowey only 1½ pence a week, 1s 9d after 70'.

In 1813 Poole built the present village school on land taken from his tanyard. It opened with eighty-five pupils, all admirably taught by Jane Turner, the daughter of an Enmore farmer who had been educated at the Enmore village school opened by the Rev John Poole. This school, too, is still in use. It was the first of its kind and became famous for its excellence. The Rev John Poole was a passionate educationalist. His book *The Village School Improved* aroused great praise so that Wordsworth wrote to Tom Poole in 1815 that he would read it, and that he rejoiced to hear of the thriving school in Nether Stowey. In Book IX of *The Excursion* he made allusion to such schools. John Poole often rode to Stowey to inspect the school's progress and at the same time in flowery lanes, by Somerset brooks, in summer fields of Cothelstone, Aisholt, the two Stoweys, pursued his other beloved employment, the study of botany, noting down the habitats of Solomon's Seal and dog's mercury, the one solitary place where wild narcissus grew, the date when he found the wild marigold in bloom. It was a pity that he never at any time fraternised with Coleridge who so loved the flowers that not long before he died he wrote 'May my eyes be closed when their beauty speaks no longer to my mind'. One of his notebooks contains a long alphabetical list of both wild and garden flowers.

In later life Tom Poole became a magistrate and dispensed justice sternly enough although several times he wrote to ask for clemency when an Assize Court had condemned a local man to some terrible penalty.

He took an unceasing interest in all affairs of Stowey church from payment of tithes to settling the singers' disputes with Dr Langford. He liked the vicar Dr Majendie so much that presents of Combwich salmon and Quantock woodcock accompanied letters written to his Windsor address. However one or two vicars found Poole opinionated and difficult. He disliked the vicar Mr Northey who became his neighbour in St Mary Street.

'I am a tanner' he always said proudly and the tanner's craft claimed his lifelong devotion. Just before Coleridge's arrival in Stowey he took, as articled apprentice, the Sherborne boy of sixteen called Thomas Ward whom Richard Poole brought home to Stowey. Young Ward hoped to become a doctor but after meeting Tom Poole he declared stoutly that he would prefer to learn the tanner's trade and to live at Poole's while learning. He became a member of the household and almost a member of the family. Coleridge liked this intelligent boy 'with the soul-beaming face' at their first meeting and ever afterwards, like Mrs Coleridge, felt warm affection for him. The Wordsworths too remembered him for years. Ward reciprocated the affection and during Coleridge's Stowey period admired him to the point of hero-worship, capering exuberantly when Poole sat holding an unopened letter from Coleridge in Germany, and willingly copying Coleridge's letters into Poole's 'copying-books' so that Poole could read them to other people. These two large notebooks with marbled paper covers contain valuable biographical material on Coleridge. The entries finish in the autumn of 1808. Several years before that date Ward became Poole's partner and by 1805 Poole withdrew from active participation in the tanning. Ward, who later married Sarah Ann Poole, granddaughter of William Poole of Shurton, became master of the Castle Street house and of the tanyard, although Poole remained the owner.

In spite of the handicaps under which the trade laboured the business extended itself. Ward and Poole became maltsters as well as tanners and ultimately timber-merchants and dealers in oak-bark.

It may be that in the early days this expansion made Poole temporarily short of money so that in 1801 he wrote to Coleridge that he could afford only part of a £50 loan. Coleridge, who already owed Poole money, replied to Poole with the most bitter and reproachful letter of their correspondence, forgetful of the countless times Poole had come to his financial rescue.

Coleridge took an interest in Poole's occupations and watched the construction of the new bark-mill during his 1807 visit. He wrote copious notes at that time about the planting and care of oaks, and after a day's basking in the sunny hayfield watching toddlers and kittens frisking among the raked 'haylines', he took down the information that layers of incompletely dried hay should be sprinkled with salt. He noted too that the cultivation of sunflowers ought to be encouraged. On Poole's behalf he passed on technical questions about the properties of oak-bark to his friend, the young Humphry Davy.

In a letter to his friend John Rickman in 1805 Poole stated that he had given up his Castle Street house to Thomas Ward 'and (I) took to this in which I now reside'. The fact that Tom Poole did not spend all his life in the Castle Street house seems to have been almost overlooked, yet he lived about thirty-five years in a second house acquired soon after his mother's death. In 1802 Tom Wedgwood wrote to him that he planned to come with Coleridge 'to see how comfortable we can make ourselves in your new house at Stowey'. (His illness prevented this.) The 1840 tithe map of Nether Stowey shows certain properties in the hands of Poole's trustees, including a house and garden unoccupied. This house, No 23 on the tithe map, was evidently Poole's home at the time of his death in 1837. Calculations and measurements identify this property with The Old House in St Mary Street. When this house and the rest of Poole's property were sold, much of his fortune was inherited by his niece Elizabeth, wife of Archdeacon Sandford. She was much loved by Tom Poole who was profoundly shocked by the death of her father when Elizabeth was a week old. Writing his *Osorio* at Stowey at about this time Coleridge reflected on this tragic situation in some lines in Scene I and was concerned to comfort Poole. He sent round a letter from his cottage to Poole in his Castle Street house: 'Shall I come to you?', fearing to intrude on Poole's grief.

Alterations and improvements to the St Mary Street house engrossed Poole for several years, with workmen coming and going and claiming his attention. Poole made himself a new bookroom, upstairs like that in Castle Street, and held out its charms as a bait to Coleridge, to induce him to spend a winter away from the north of England:

> Come and pass it here. I have made a nice, very nice, *bookroom* in which *you may regulate the climate as you like*, in which there is even a bed though you can't see it. I promise to get any books you want.

Undoubtedly Coleridge spent many hours reading in this pleasant room during his visits in 1803 and 1807. He borrowed from its shelves the old German book *Todten Tanz* bought by Poole in Basle, took it away with him and sent it back years later with his own epitaph written on the flyleaf:

> Here lies a Poet—or what once was He;
> Pray, gentle Reader, pray for S.T.C.,
> That he who threescore years with toilsome breath
> Found death in life, may now find life in death:
> Mercy for praise, *to be forgiven*, for fame,
> He asked, and hoped, thro' Christ.
> Do thou the same.

Three years after moving in, Poole was still busy improving this favourite room, and writing to friends that they would find it much more comfortable now that he had installed a 'wooden tunnel' to cure its smoky chimney. Like Coleridge he had an obsession with altering chimneys; somewhat enviously he looked across at the 'turnabout' and weather-vane erected on one of the vicarage chimneys. He had planted tall shrubs under the book room window to hide what he called the most unpleasant part of the stables just across the courtyard.

Perhaps a writing-table in this library of Poole's contained what Mrs Coleridge called 'a few things of S.T.C.'s writing' when she wrote to ask Poole, as late as 1832, to find them and send them on for a new edition of Coleridge's poems that his son-in-law Henry Nelson Coleridge was preparing. (Coleridge's daughter married a cousin.) Coleridge and his wife had, of course, long lived apart. 'Republishing the Poems is his own concern, only he is so dilatory he will never do it without help.'

Right up till the end of his life Tom Poole did anything he could that might help Coleridge or his family.

This book room, 'this delicious room' as Penelope Anstice called it, remained Poole's pride and joy. De Quincey felt astonished that a plain, old-fashioned farmer owned the wealth of books he found on its shelves and on those of its little ante-room. In the 1830s a copy of Coleridge's portrait by Allston hung on a wall in company with one of Humphry Davy. The mantelpiece displayed a great treasure: one of the few Wedgwood copies of the Berberini vase, presented to Poole by his friends Josiah and Thomas.

How many distinguished men, besides Coleridge and De Quincey, became familiar with this room! Southey; John Kenyon, the Brownings' friend, who lived at Woodlands House, Holford —often mentioned by Dorothy Wordsworth—and who became a friend of the Coleridges when they lived away from Somerset; Andrew Crosse, squire of Broomfield and a noted scientist; Humphry Davy whose last visit was made when he was mortally ill, 'the wreck of what I was'; Billingsley, who wrote the *Survey of Somerset Agriculture* and came to dine in Easter week off a sirloin from Poole's prize ox; Lord Egmont; John Rickman; Josiah Wedgwood.

The carriage entrance of The Old House opens directly on to St Mary Street and the stables stand just inside. The stables have two floors and each possesses a fireplace used perhaps for making a hot mash for the horses after a long, cold journey. The fire would warm the stable-men who slept on the upper floor, including the unpopular William who, Mrs Coleridge condescendingly said, 'made an excellent charioteer'. The book room is still entered by a small ante-room. The dormer windows above its window belong to the attics where the servants slept as in the Castle Street house.

This house has a less imposing façade than that of the Castle Street house and nobody passing by would guess how charming a dwelling it is. The square hall, with its nice staircase turning at right-angles halfway up, opens on the left into Poole's attractive parlour beneath the book room. This room looks on to the street where Poole could see his familiar Stowey brook running past in its pebbled channel and overflowing in heavy rain. The wall at the fireplace-end has eighteenth-century panelling of dark oak. In Poole's time Raeburn's portrait of his idolised niece Elizabeth Sandford hung in this room and in his later years its furniture included a piano that she played on when she came from Edinburgh or Dunchurch to stay. She was a talented and well-educated young woman whose energy amazed Mrs Coleridge, and woke envy in the gifted but delicate young Sara.

High walls of red sandstone still enclose the very big and beautiful garden extending to glebe land that the bypass now cuts across, although Poole wrote that he contemplated partly demolishing them. In this garden during the summer of 1807 Coleridge found seclusion and solitude. During part of that summer his children played here, enjoying sunny hours they remembered when older: Hartley, so charming, so much adored, who grew up to cause such disappointment and worry—'my poor Hartley' Mrs Coleridge called him in letters to Poole; fat, placid Derwent whom Coleridge had wanted to call Thomas Poole but named differently because the other name would offend Poole relatives; Sara, the 'sweet, animated fairy' (as Poole described her) in her miniature mob-cap. Years later Sara came with her husband Henry Coleridge and in spite of the illness she suffered whilst in Somerset, eagerly showed him places known to her father.

Poole helped Hartley with money when he was an undergraduate and invited him to Nether Stowey during vacation. He regarded the boy as his godson. Before Hartley's visit in 1817 Poole wrote enthusiastically to Coleridge that he would show the boy every brook, hill, dale and 'the old apple tree bent earthward' in the Lime Street cottage garden. 'Old Mrs Rich will leap for joy', he wrote, referring to the old woman who had sometimes done jobs at the cottage. Perhaps Hartley got bored by Poole's enthusiastic reminiscences of his father's youth.

No wife ever graced this house of Tom Poole's. In his twenties he fell in love with his cousin at Marsh Mill House, dark-eyed Penelope who sang so sweetly that Tom wooed her with clumsy verses in which he swore her voice surpassed the song of the nightingale in the lane at Marshmills. But Penelope could not imagine cousin Tom as her lover; neither could the girl he approached a few years after.

In 1797 he met Josiah and Thomas Wedgwood, wealthy sons of the great Staffordshire potter, at their brother's house near Bristol. Josiah remained his lifelong friend, a cultured, philanthropic man who was also hard-headed and business-like. Tom gave both Poole and Coleridge his affectionate friendship until his untimely death in 1805 from the intestinal malady that perpetually shadowed his life without undermining the courage and sweetness of his disposition. His great talent for chemistry helped him to master the printing of 'silver pictures' that earned him the title of 'the first photographer'. He came to Castle Street as Poole's guest in 1797, met Coleridge, and fell so completely under the spell of his genius that he persuaded Josiah to an act of supreme generosity towards the impoverished poet. Several times Coleridge enjoyed hospitality from the Wedgwoods. However when he travelled from Stowey with Tom Poole in February 1803, to enjoy a holiday at Josiah Wedgwood's home at Tarrant Gunville in Dorset, he did not know what feelings Kitty Wedgwood (Josiah's sister Catherine) nurtured towards him and which she had just forcibly expressed in a letter to her brother Tom, also on his way to Dorset. She told him that while *he* himself should have a warm, pleasant bedroom and while Mr Coleridge's should be comfortable, she would give Mr Coleridge a room in the tower; 'not smart' as 'we shall never agree respecting this gentleman' whose accent and appearance had from the first given her a disagreeable impression and whom she disliked for his conceit and his 'parade of superior feeling'. She considered him an uncomfortable husband and a negligent father who would expect others to provide at his death.

Page 53 (left) Castle Street, Nether Stowey, showing the brook; the opening by the wall *(left)* is Tanyard Lane;

(right) Tom Poole's house, Castle Street. Behind the shop window is the parlour where Poole entertained Coleridge and Wordsworth

Manor Mill House at Over Stowey, the home of Tom Poole's uncle and cousins

Two years before this visit Poole had written to ask if he might correspond with this same candid Kitty, with a view to matrimony. Her brother wrote back to pass on her forceful refusal. Poor Poole said 'I was stunned by it though I do not know why, and I stood looking at it for an hour'.

In spite of the Wedgwoods' radical principles even Tom said that 'Poole's witless presumption' astonished him, and sturdy Tom Poole humbly admitted that he had been presumptuous. Kitty may have been put off by his total lack of polish, for by some freak of obstinacy he clung to rustic roughness in speech and person— Coleridge said 'There is not one fault in his dialect he ever got rid of'—just as he opposed such extravagances as powdering the hair. This antipathy to hair-powder caused Coleridge's seemingly impolite letter to Poole in which, after visiting Sarah King, he teasingly asked whether Poole's sister had caught some complaint in the head as her hair was filled with *odious white dandruff*.

However Poole suffered a shattering disappointment when he failed to obtain for the Wedgwoods Mr Francis Gwyn's manor house at Combe Florey, a pretty village set among red ploughlands within sight of the Quantocks. When he wrote to Coleridge in Germany to break the news of his baby son's death he told him, astonishingly, to refrain from immense grief since 'I myself have experienced disappointment more weighty than the death of 10 infants'—meaning that these friends would now have to settle further away from Stowey. Poole often exhorted Coleridge not to worry about *anything*, not even his wife and family, lest he impede the development of his powers. Poole thought the worries might easily be carried by Mrs Coleridge, and indeed many of them were.

During their earliest meetings Coleridge dazzled him, an effect he had on many people during those three years when his genius burned so brightly. After Coleridge's visit to Stowey in September 1795 Poole wrote some lines as bad as those he addressed to Penelope.

> Hail to thee Coldridge, youth of various powers!
> I love to hear thy soul pour forth the line,
> To hear it sing of love and liberty
> As if fresh-breathing from the hand divine.

D

The passing years stripped Poole, like the Wordsworths, of all illusions about Coleridge's character and made him see the developing weaknesses fatal to any achievement comparable with that of his Stowey period. However, again like the Wordsworths, he loved the ill-starred poet to the end of his life.

Poole died in 1837. The great crowd at his funeral heard his niece's husband, Archdeacon Sandford, speak eloquently of the service he had rendered men of all ranks in his native town and beyond. Coleridge had paid tribute to his friend some years earlier when he wrote a magnificent appreciation of Tom Poole in the periodical *Church and State*.

CHAPTER 3

FIRST VISITS; CLEVEDON;
THE ADSCOMBE PROJECT

During his summer vacation from Cambridge in 1794 Coleridge made the acquaintance of Robert Southey, an undergraduate from Balliol whom he joined on a walking tour in Wales. Southey won his admiration and esteem; he was a 'nightingale among owls'. The son of a Bristol draper and grandson of a farmer at Lydeard St Lawrence near the Quantocks, he lived according to a strict moral code that influenced Coleridge into reforming his own sexual behaviour. At the same time he awoke in Coleridge an almost fanatical enthusiasm for his project of founding a pantisocracy. This, in brief, was a scheme for finding 'twelve men and twelve ladies' who would emigrate to settle on the banks of the Susquehanna, and found a Utopian community, pooling their financial resources. Their first young adherent was Robert Lovell who was engaged to Mary Fricker, one of five sisters who supported themselves and their mother by their needlework. Coleridge met the Fricker family in Bath where Southey had taken him to stay with his mother. Later, Southey married Edith Fricker, but Coleridge, for the time being, paid only flirtatious attention to her sister Sara as he was deeply in love with a girl called Mary Evans. He wrote his poem 'The Sigh' for Mary when later in the year she rejected him because the pantisocratic scheme did not attract her. Sara, however, would have promised to go to the banks of the Susquehanna or anywhere else at that time if it ensured marriage to the fascinating poet whom in a few years time she was to compare enviously with the more reliable Southey, her brother-in-law. Coleridge himself mentioned Bath in conversation with an acquaintance years later and added, 'and there I had the misfortune to meet my wife'.

On a July day he set out from Bath with Southey on a long Somerset walk, taking in Cheddar, Wells, Huntspill, Bridgwater and, finally, Nether Stowey. Poetry and the pantisocratic scheme filled their heads. They talked of both with excitement as they walked between the dust-powdered green hedges or sprawled at the open wayside among sun-bleached grasses. This trunk road to the west, that for over ten miles of their route from Bath followed the Fosse Way so straightly ruled by the Romans, swept across Norton Down, part of the rock-boned range of Mendip, to fall downward to the tiny village of Chilcompton which Collinson called 'a little parish on the great turnpike road to Wells and Bridgwater'. When Coleridge and Southey tramped along the trunk road it did indeed pass through the steep narrow valley that cradled the village before ascending to Old Down, but the later turnpike road did not penetrate the combe, the birthplace of the old village as its name explains, nor does the present Bath—Well road although the modern development of Chilcompton lies along it.

Coleridge's mind hardly registered Chilcompton's name. Only a year later he wrote the title 'Lines addressed to a Spring in Village of Kirkhampton, near Bath' on one page of the manuscript of a sheaf of youthful poems that he gave to Mrs Estlin. Yet the charm of the pretty sequestered place where they paused in July heat to drink the 'milky waters cold and clear' exerted itself strongly enough to make him write some verses whose final title became 'Lines to a Beautiful Spring in a Village'. The main feature of the village is still the impetuous rivulet Somer (a fairly modern name that hurries along on the east side of the street in the combe, filling the air with its silvery voice. It charmed Coleridge just as it had charmed Collinson who wrote that it abounded with trout and eels, that it had its source at the head of the valley where several springs gushed out near 'romantick shaggy rocks', and that its descent through the village was intercepted by many artificial falls. These miniature cascades dropping over stone steps create swirls of foam that whiten the clear current, as Coleridge observed. The

stream grows broad and very fast where it sweeps under a culvert.
Bushes and tree-branches, on which children climb, overhang it.
It grows swifter still as it approaches the village school. A top
railing is designed as part-protection, but one sees children turning somersaults on it or going through the gaps where little steps
lead down to the stream in order to sail plastic boats or bits of
wood, just as Coleridge saw them 'with infant uproar . . . released
from school' launching 'paper navies' on its breast. We can still
see the place Coleridge saw in spite of the railway line, the prefabs,
the ruined dwellings of grey Mendip stone that he must have seen
in use, and nineteenth-century rebuilding of the church reached
by the narrow path called The Pitching. The L-shaped Tudor
manor-house still stands by the church; its mill was working
briskly when Coleridge came. Alongside the village street fine
houses survive from Coleridge's day: Eagle House with the stone
eagle over the doorway, Shell House with shell hood protecting its
door, Gainsborough House with stone-mullioned windows. On the
stream's east bank he saw stately Norton Hall that was demolished
and effaced in the nineteenth century except for the shells of grim
stone dwellings once occupied by its servants. Coleridge's attention
was caught by a girl loitering with her pitcher in time-honoured
fashion by the cascading stream to talk with a man from a farm
who leaned on his sheep-crook—at least, so his poem says.

From Chilcompton he and Southey walked to Cheddar where,
on a stifling July night, they had to share a single bed on which
Coleridge tossed so restlessly that Southey termed him a vile
bedfellow. A breath of Mendip air must have fanned through
the casement, bearing a whiff of fragrance from the roses and
woodbine growing in gardens of the grey or whitewashed stone
cottages. The village, pretty as a picture in a fairytale, straggled
away from the foot of the gorge where no carriage-road had yet
been laid, but where a broad boulder-strewn track wound breath-
lessly upward. Women sat on the steps of the village Market Cross
to sell eggs and butter, shaded by the open-arched hexagonal
stone structure that was growing dilapidated and would be restored
(to its present state) in the century following.

Living conditions in this village were anything but idyllic and
growing harsher with the progress of enclosure that would soon

include the rich green common where Defoe had found every man pasturing his cows. Modest self-sufficiency had turned in many instances to intense poverty on a wage of 14d per day or parish relief. Hannah More, whom Coleridge met later in Bristol, said she found Cheddar people as ignorant and un-Christian as inhabitants of Africa. Here she started her Mendip Bible schools and met the opposition of Cheddar farmers whose hearts, where their labourers' education was concerned, were stony as the heart of Mendip. Coleridge can have grasped little of this as his was a fleeting visit. He paid another in 1798 with the Wordsworths. What could not have failed to make him marvel at first sight was the spectacular scenery towering above the village. In one of his letters he described how sublimity in natural scenery, such features as mountains, precipices, torrents, filled him with awe. Here he saw nine crystalline springs bursting from the foot of the cliffs and joining to form the clear and rapid river called Cheddar Water that ran over a bed of sand and shingle, with small rocks breaking its surface. Its movement and its little waterfalls kept the ferns on its brink a-quiver. Trout and roach swam in the water and on the rocks limpets clung, shaped like a truncated cone, amber and blue in colour with stripes of purple. Seven mills were worked by this stream, three of them for papermaking. It flowed away across the green moors to join the river Axe that wound through unmeasured caverns.

Walking the track that led up the gorge for over a mile Coleridge felt himself a pygmy as he craned up at overhanging giant cliffs of rough grey and pinkish rock, shaggy with bushes and cushioned at intervals by masses of summer-faded wild pinks. Almost certainly he looked into one of the five vaulted caves where someone carried a candle to reveal the gleaming of jagged stalactites and crystallisations, and told him that the cliffs and rock-ribbed hillsides were honeycombed with such places, dark and unexplored. They shouted to make the echoes reverberate. At the summit of the gorge he set foot on rough Mendip land, hundreds of acres in extent, swept by winds, strewn with stone, bumpy with long barrows. Sheep browsed on the grass, and any shepherd he spoke to would show him swallet-holes in the ground through which lambs sometimes dropped. If he knelt to look down one of these, the weird noises of underground waters reached his ears. If he went into one of the woods hanging on a hillside, perhaps he saw a great coil of intertwined adders like those still found there on beds of dead leaves.

It would be an exaggeration to imply that Coleridge's great fantasy-poem 'Kubla Khan' had its genesis in the impression made by his first sight of Cheddar and Mendip landscape; the origins of the images that surged up before him in his daylight dream at Porlock have been too thoroughly explored by every effort of meticulous scholarship for such a suggestion to possess substance. Yet 'that deep romantic chasm', the caves of ice, the river running 'through caverns measureless to man down to a sunless sea' are not unlike glorified, magnified versions of the gorge, the cave glittering with stalactites, the underground river Axe mentioned in some eighteenth-century lines about the Cheddar river that Collinson quoted after surveying it:

> And Cheddar . . .
> Gusht forth to forcefull streams, that he was like to break
> The greater bankes of Axe, as from his mother's cave
> He wandered towards the sea.

Afterwards the two friends walked along the foot of Mendip through Draycott and Rodney Stoke to Wells, following more or less the line of the present A371 road. From Wells they walked to Huntspill, through Wedmore, Blackford, Mark, to Highbridge, along a road that is now the B3139 which at Highbridge joins the A38, the road from Bristol. They took this road with which Coleridge would grow so familiar during the next three years, to reach the village of Huntspill where they visited George Burnett, fellow-student with Southey at Balliol and an ardent recruit for the pantisocracy scheme. Coleridge had already met him during an Oxford visit when he struck up an intimate friendship with this talented and unsatisfactory young man. The Burnetts were an old Huntspill family and George Burnett's father farmed many of the surrounding flat lush fields. He rented some of his rich grazing land from Paul Methuen whose famous collection of pictures at Corsham Coleridge would visit as a guest a few years later.

After the Huntspill visit Coleridge and Southey walked to

Bridgwater via Pawlett, Puriton Hill and Crandon Bridge, a road Monmouth's waggons had used, and then a final eight miles to Nether Stowey. The long pedestrian journey from Bath had cost them little except the price of a bed in Cheddar. It is interesting to see how expensive the Stowey—Bath journey was when Coleridge made it, in reverse, in January 1802 by post-chaise and kept an account. The stages were Stowey to Bridgwater; Bridgwater to Piper's Inn on the Polden Hills; Piper's Inn to Wells; Wells to Old Down; Old Down to Bath. Charges for the chaise were: 11s 3d, 13s 1½d, 13s 1½d, 8s 9d, 16s 3d, while each time the driver received 2s 6d and the turnpike charge was 6d.

Southey wrote later that they went to Stowey to meet a friend of Coleridge's. There is no evidence that Tom Poole had ever met Coleridge before this summer visit in 1794. The friend Coleridge went to visit was Henry Poole, a fellow-undergraduate at Jesus College and cousin to Tom Poole. Probably he was the Henry Poole who became Vicar of Cannington a few years later and for whom Tom Poole wrote a successful sermon, full of patriotic fervour, in 1803 when England was at war. Henry Poole, who went up to Cambridge in 1791, was a scholar and an exhibitioner 'son of William (farmer) deceased, of Nether Stowey'. His grandfather William Poole was a very well-off farmer living at Shurton, a coastal hamlet in the parish of Stogursey, not far from the site of the modern nuclear power station called Hinkley Point. This William Poole farmed land in Stogursey, Fiddington and at Stowey where he rented part of the land pertaining to Stowey Farm. It is highly probable that Henry Poole entertained Coleridge and Southey during their short stay in the summer of 1794 at his grandfather's home Shurton Court. During the next two years Coleridge referred familiarly in his letters to 'Bill Poole of Shurton' and to 'Bill Poole's large house'. In November 1796 he wrote to Tom Poole (William Poole's nephew) that he would send him Burke's pamphlet 'inclosed in a parcel to Bill Poole of Shurton'. Tom Poole wrote that he had heard much of Coleridge before ever he met him in 1794. He could have heard about him at that time only from George Burnett or from this young cousin Henry Poole.

Shurton Court is a fine three-storeyed Georgian house greatly in need of restoration and now divided into flats. Great swags of ivy overhang the half-crumbling blue lias walls of its overgrown garden. If Henry Poole and his visitors went for a stroll when the August evening cooled, they came to a noisy little stream flowing close to the high garden-wall, and stood talking on one of its three hump-backed bridges, watching the wagtails on the stones of the shallow ford. This corner of Shurton has not changed.

Shurton Court housed a large family, some of them still young. There were Anne, Harriet, Sophia, Charles, and Lavinia who became Mrs Draper. In spring 1798 Coleridge wrote for Lavinia his verses 'To a Young Lady on her Recovery from a Fever', although he addressed her as 'Louisa dear' in his poem. Perhaps Lavinia went through a bout of typhoid like many people in the locality at that time.

Henry Poole brought Coleridge and Southey to Tom's house in Stowey. From the first, Tom fell completely under the spell of the lively impassioned student he called 'Coldridge' and felt eager to introduce him to his much-loved Marshmills cousins, particularly John Poole who was now a Fellow of Oriel and spent most of his time at his family home, reading for Holy Orders. Coleridge, the 'shining scholar', had impressed Poole with his 'splendid abilities', the 'elegance and energy and uncommon facility' with which he spoke. He had swiftly confided to Poole that he meant to reform his conduct, that in religion he was a Unitarian and in politics an extreme Democrat—which practically meant a revolutionary. Moreover he had recruited Poole as a supporter for the project of founding an egalitarian community in the backwoods of America. What did he look like at this time when the people of Nether Stowey and Over Stowey first set eyes on him? He was twenty-two. Three years later Dorothy Wordsworth described him thus:

At first I thought him very plain, that is for about 3 minutes. He is pale and thin, has a wide mouth, thick lips, not very good teeth, longish, loose-growing half-curling rough black hair. But if you hear him speak for 5 minutes you think no more of them.

His eye is large and full, not dark but grey, such an eye as would receive from a heavy soul the dullest expression, but it speaks every motion of his animated mind; it has more of the poet's eye in a fine frenzy rolling than I ever witnessed.

He has dark eyebrows and an overhanging forehead.

Tom Poole ingenuously believed that his scholarly cousin John, conventional, God-fearing, and an unalterable Tory, would take great pleasure in meeting this high-spirited and original friend of cousin Henry Poole. That morning John Poole had walked up the lane to Over Stowey to borrow Boswell's *Life of Johnson* from his friend Mr Lewis the curate and at one o'clock sat peacefully reading it in a room looking out on the Quantock Hills. The garden gate clicked, conversation and laughter reached his ears, five young men came up the path. The interruption itself irritated him. He did not feel very cordial at that moment towards his cousin Tom whose reckless political views had earned considerable local comment, nor towards Tom's brother Richard, the youthful doctor on holiday from Sherborne, who had lately been called 'a flaming Democrat', nor, at this moment, to Henry Poole. He felt still less cordial towards the two talkative strangers they had brought along at this inconvenient hour just before dinner. He greeted them with stiff courtesy. Their excited talk and laughter engulfed him. Their discussion grew hotter and more excited while his own manner became stiffer and colder—as they noticed, so that the mischievous desire to shock took possession of both Coleridge and Southey. And shock him they did with their hot-headed talk and alarming opinions, above all with their exaggerated expressions of grief over the recent death of Robespierre. That night he wrote in his journal, his hand still shaking with indignation, that the two strangers were both atheists and 'shamefully hot with Democratic rage as regards politics'. His unfavourable opinions of Tom's friends and his disapproval of Tom's judgement had been confirmed that same evening by Mr Reekes, a Stowey schoolmaster or tutor, who called on him about seven o'clock to tell him that he had been absolutely appalled by the odious views expressed by two young men encountered that afternoon at Tom Poole's house.

John Poole's dislike of Coleridge remained ineradicable, like his sharp-tongued sister's. Over the years he met him in Tom's

company a number of times but never changed his hostile attitude.
Sixty years later Cornelia Crosse, the chatelaine of Fyne Court at
Broomfield, not far from Enmore, was paying a morning call on
the Trevelyans at Enmore Castle. Mrs Crosse, who greatly loved
the poetry of Coleridge and Wordsworth and who eagerly collected all the associations available, was delighted to find that
another caller at the castle, the aged and almost saintly rector of
Enmore, had known the poets personally. She buttonholed the
Rev John Poole with eagerness and drew out his memories of
Coleridge and Wordsworth in their youth, reminding him of the
local prejudice and ignorance that had led Quantock people to
campaign against them. His reaction horrified her. She found
that this venerable, educated man had shared the stupid prejudices
and harboured the same dislike. 'Even the lapse of half a century
had not removed the warp from his mind.' Grudgingly he admitted that the two men *had* become very distinguished but, he added,
'Coleridge especially talked sad democratic nonsense when I used
to meet him at Tom Poole's'.

Back to Bath, and an incredibly ill-considered engagement to
Sara Fricker. Return to Cambridge supposedly for another year
but in reality for only one term during which he wrote a number
of poems that included 'On a Discovery made too Late', written
after receiving a letter from Mary Evans. She told him she loved
him, but, as he said, it was too late, or so he believed. When he
sent the poem to Southey he promised, 'Mark you, Southey, I will
do my duty'. He became friendly with Charles Lamb. By December
he was in Bristol where he began his extensive borrowings from
the Public Library which was the delightful building in King
Street, designed by Paty. He bought the Memorandum book now
called the *Gutch Notebook* and in the New Year started filling it
with notes and jottings of all kinds that he continued to scribble
in this same notebook for three years. In Bristol he made several
lifelong friends who included Josiah Wade, later a witness at his
wedding; the Rev Mr Estlin, Unitarian minister; Joseph Cottle
who became the publisher of his poems as well as publisher of
those Wordsworth wrote at Alfoxden; the Morgans who owned
a cottage at Box, near Bath, where he lived for a time years later.

Coleridge lodged at 48 College Street, as did Southey and

George Burnett; their heads still seethed with plans for the pantisocracy. Coleridge was soon in money difficulties. Kind Cottle lent money to pay his lodgings bill as well as George Burnett's, and to Coleridge's joy offered him 30 guineas for the copyright of a volume of poems. Coleridge undertook delivering a series of lectures; some were given at the Corn Market, some at a coffee-house. Tom Poole received a prospectus and attended one or two. Cottle then offered Coleridge the payment of $1\frac{1}{2}$ guineas for every hundred lines of poetry he wrote. He very soon found that Coleridge often wished to anticipate payment and that he vexed Mr Biggs the printer by failing to send his copy at promised dates.

Coleridge, however, feeling himself fairly launched, and on this narrow, spasmodic income, turned his thoughts to marriage. Sara Fricker with her widowed mother now lived at Redcliffe Hill and he saw her frequently, taking her for walks round Bristol as Southey did her sister Edith. By this time he had persuaded him-self that he was in love with her. She was twenty-one, petite, blue-eyed, plump, fresh-looking, dotingly in love with him, delightful to embrace and kiss. The prospect of more sensual joys excited him for he had a warm and passionate nature. He could scarcely have chosen a girl less likely to satisfy him either physically or intellectually, and even a girl well-endowed with passion and intellect would have found it a hard task to make marriage to Coleridge a success.

And so the poems written early in 1795 are shot tenderly and sentimentally with Sara's name, and at times express in flowery, metaphorical terms his impatience to rest upon 'the bosom of my love'. His poem 'To the Rev W. J. Hort While Teaching a Young Lady some Song-Tunes on his Flute' is addressed to a friend who was teaching Sara by this method. Its reference to future wander-ings with her 'Up the rude romantic glen, Up the cliff and thro' the glade' imply that Coleridge already had his eye on the Clevedon cottage. In May he went walking on Mendip and wrote a poem that, like the Chilcompton poem, owed its inspiration entirely to a Somerset scene. That day he had climbed the steep side of Brockley Combe and as he referred in his poem to the left ascent he must have approached the combe from the direction of Brockley village, then a small, hidden place of 173 inhabitants and 19 houses that included Brockley Hall and Brockley Manor close to the church. Even today the path to the church turns off the traffic-ridden Bristol—Weston-super-Mare road to run through a huge cornfield where the sound of the wind in the trees blurs the noise of traffic. The romantic ravine, as the passage through the combe was described in the early years of the nineteenth century, extends for over a mile from the entrance Coleridge used at the side of the Bristol—Weston road, to open on the present A38 near Lulsgate or Bristol Airport, at a point where Brockley Combe is named on the signpost. The road through the combe carries plenty of traffic today but is still a haven of green shade on a hot summer after-noon. In Coleridge's time it was described as a fine gravel road 'terminating on heathery downs'. He turned aside from this road and climbed, with considerable exertion, the limestone crags of the south-eastern side that had hawthorns in snowy bloom, dark yews and other trees twined with ivy rooted in their fissures, and coloured mosses growing on their surface. Seated on a slab of lime-stone, he gazed over a pastoral landscape. He gave his little landscape-poem a cumbersome title: 'Lines, Composed while climbing the Left Ascent of Brockley Coomb in Somersetshire.'

That year he paid several visits to Tom Poole and firmly cemented the friendship. Charlotte Poole of Marsh Mill House met Coleridge at her cousin Tom's in September and wrote in her journal: 'Tom Poole has a friend with him of the name of Coldridge; a young man of brilliant understanding, great eloquence, desperate fortune, democratick principles and entirely led away by the feelings of the moment'. It was a fairly shrewd assessment of Coleridge, if unfriendly. During this visit he saw Tom Poole inventing recipes for making a cheap loaf as the price of bread had reached a desperate level for the Stowey poor.

Coleridge spent part of this September visit with the Pooles at Shurton Court. Seven years later he wrote from St Clear in Carmarthen that the country around was bleak and dreary 'such as the country round Shurton'. The farmlands here are rich and pastoral, tufted with woods and backed by the undulating range of the Quantocks, but the pewter-grey Bristol Channel and grey-brown stony beaches certainly convey an impression of dreariness on a day without sunshine. Yet he remembered the place with a certain affection when in Germany, wishing his boat might put in at Shurton Bars (where there was no harbour, the nearest being a small and dangerously rocky one at Lilstock, mainly for boats carrying limestone). Going up the river at Cuxhaven he noticed the uneven banks striated with lines of green and remembered the sea-banks at Shurton.

His poem headed: 'Lines Written at Shurton Bars near Bridge-water, September 1795' makes clear that he found his way down to the coast by a road that is still almost as remote and unfrequented. In the tiny twin hamlet called Burton a lane by the post office runs between hedges thick with elder-trees to end on a corner by the stone farmhouse of Knighton Farm that stood there in Coleridge's time like the primitive, thick walled, stone-floored empty cottage situated on the opposite side of the road and recently occupied by an old hermit. To the left of the farm a rough cart-track runs towards the sea, and for a while a stream flagged with yellow iris and shallowing to make a little ford runs alongside it before branching through a field. Meanwhile the cart-track runs on to loop over three large humps and climb to high, windy fields full of sheep and looking out to sea. In spring it is shrill with the songs of skylarks and Coleridge's poem refers in one place to skylarks settling in nests amid the summer corn and nodding poppies. He was here early in September. The sheep-field is bounded by a wire fence where its side falls steeply to the shore. If Coleridge stood here today he would see westward, on the left, the familiar cliff-side displaying strata of yellow sandstone and blue lias with intervening thin green strips of grass. The cliffs curve away towards the headland jutting out from Minehead. Nearer to view, the tamarisks used for dyeing by the Quantock weavers make a hedge level with the Lilstock shore. Eastward, a farm, brown ploughland—and the great towers of Hinkley Point nuclear power station rising near the place where Coleridge saw a ruined house.

From the field edge he looked down on piles of brown and grey shinglestones planed smooth by the sea; on a strip of grey-brown sand strewn with black seaweeds; on a shining silver-grey tide sweeping 'with mimic thunders' over the rolling shingle under a cloudless sky. Looking straight out across the sea he saw the two islands, Flat Holm like a floating raft and Steep Holm rising abruptly from the water, while far to the right Brean Down plunged into the sea at the end of Mendip and Crook's Peak drew its faint, hooked outline. It was 'the channelled Isle' of Flat Holm that held his eye. Today anyone looking towards it sees the white column of its lighthouse. Coleridge saw the stone pillar, erected in 1737, crowned by the redly blazing watchfire or beacon that warned sailors of the reefs.

Some time that September he had met William Wordsworth at the Pinneys' house in Bristol. He read Wordsworth's poem 'An Evening Walk' and copied from it—as he himself acknowledged —the expression 'green radiance' used in the 'Lines Written at Shurton Bars' when he described glow-worms shining on the banks of Shurton lanes. It is not a poem of great quality. Its sub-title is 'In Answer to a Letter from Bristol', and its final stanzas speak of the ecstasy he anticipated from marriage with Sara, from holding her to his heart on some stormy midnight when she would weep for those in danger from the elements. Once more he was thinking of the cottage at Clevedon, set within hearing of the sea. He took Sara Fricker there as his bride after their marriage in St Mary Redcliffe on 4 October 1795. He had secured the cottage by mid-August when he wrote a more exquisite poem than 'Shurton Bars' after sitting in the cottage garden with Sara beside him lean-ing her cheek on his arm.

CLEVEDON

He called it the valley of seclusion and that is exactly what it was in 1795. Today it is difficult to imagine that this description ever fitted Clevedon. The town lies 15 miles from Bristol whence it is approached by taking the B3128 road in the Weston-super-Mare direction and by travelling through Failand and Tickenham. Much of this route is beautiful. Acres of fields shining with butter-cups in spring, and miles of greyish-pink garden walls and park-walls overtopped by fine beeches, border the road. The eye is filled by an immense sweep of blue and green landscape with woods hanging on the slopes of the long hill stretching from

Tickenham, with farms and their buildings of grey stone. But nearer Clevedon a seemingly endless line of bungalows has extended under the hanging woods and the hidden prehistoric Cadbury Camp (known as Cadbury-Tickenham and not to be confused with the supposed site of Camelot). The twentieth century has added Edwardian villas, modern houses, bungalows, shops, garages—including the big garage Austin House opposite Coleridge's dwelling—and a murderous flow of traffic that passes noisily through Coleridge's valley of seclusion where the nineteenth century had already put hotels, a seaside pier, a railway-station and many imposing Italianate and Gothic villas of grey stone built to cling like huge molluscs to the green, rock-strewn hill-slopes Coleridge knew. Even by 1840 the population numbered little more than 1,100, and, Coleridge's little grey fishing village could not have held more than a quarter of that number.

It sheltered beneath the long, rocky height called Dial Hill, at its western extremity. It consisted of a handful of thatched and tiled stone cottages—a few of these survive—built at some distance from the parish church of St Andrew that dominates Clevedon Pill and whose tower, squat as it is, was a familiar mark to sailors out in the bay. This ancient church stands high, bowered in trees and on one side overlooking an expanse of Somerset landscape that includes the sullen blue wave of Mendip. Strong winds and exceptionally high spring tides beat the Clevedon coast, yet the air is soft and mild enough to cherish myrtle, arbutus and delicate shrubs in many gardens, as advertisements for the nineteenth-century watering-place informed potential visitors and as Coleridge's Clevedon poems proclaim. In 'The Eolian Harp' and in 'Reflections on Having Left a Place of Retirement' he mentioned the myrtles blossoming in his garden, the white jasmine twining over his porch, the rose that climbed to their bedroom-window. A neighbouring bean-field contributed its scent in late evening when 'the stilly murmur of the distant sea' reached their ears. They heard the sea's faint murmur the minute they woke; you would not hear it now if you stood outside his cottage, only the noise of traffic. He always referred to his Clevedon home, rented at £5 per annum, as 'our pretty cot': it is still pretty, and in its time has been called Rose Cottage and Myrtle Cottage. Its present postal

Page 71 (left) Portrait of Coleridge painted in 1795 by van Dyke, when Coleridge was living at Clevedon;

(right) William Wordsworth, from an early portrait in the Tite collection of Taunton Castle

Page 72 Coleridge's cottage in Lime Street, Nether Stowey; the end building is an addition

designation is 55 Old Church Road, and an inconspicuous plaque on its wall states that 'Samuel Taylor Coleridge spent his honeymoon in this cottage in 1795'.

It is one of a pair of cottages sheltering below the trees and rocks of steep Dial Hill, a stone cottage with a redbrick chimney, a roof of red pantiles and a brick porch with a timber gable. Roses no longer climb to the tiny bedroom windows nor does jasmine wreathe the porch, but fuchsias in bloom at the side of its flagged path testify to the mildness of the air as truthfully as Coleridge's myrtles. A big tree slants its greenery across the adjoining white cottage and the boughs of beeches wave behind the roofs. Traditionally this is Coleridge's honeymoon house, his 'pretty cot' that remained one of his sweetest memories, yet a small doubt exists concerning the authenticity of its claims. Joseph Cottle who visited the Coleridges a few days after their wedding wrote in his *Recollections* that the cottage was 'but one story high'. It is true that he wrote this many years afterwards but the statement corresponds in some degree with Coleridge's lines: 'Low was our pretty cot: our tallest Rose Peeped at the chamber-window'.

If Coleridge's cottage had only one storey it was not this house unless it has been rebuilt. Unfortunately access to the interior of this cottage is not easy to obtain as it is private property.

Cottle greatly admired the little house, enjoyed his stay, found the young couple very happy. He thought the whitewashed parlour lacking in comfort and kindly sent a Bristol decorator to paper it with patterned wallpaper. His generosity had already supplied the Coleridges with a varied assortment of goods from Bristol shops requested by Coleridge two days after the marriage.

A riddle slice; a candle box, two ventilators; two glasses for the wash-hand stand; one tin dust pan; one small tin tea kettle; one pair of candlesticks; one carpet brush; one flower (flour) dredge; three tin extinguishers; two mats; a pair of slippers; a cheese toaster; two large tin spoons; a bible; a keg of porter; coffee; raisins; currants; catsup; nutmegs; allspice; cinnamon; rice; ginger and mace.

Nor were these all the articles lacked by the Coleridge house-

E

hold. Coleridge made another list, headed *Desiderata*, in his note-book, the items of which included:

1 Set of better China
2 Tubs and a Pail
4 Urine Pots
2 beds
4 blankets
5 pair Sheets of the finer order
2 pair for Servant
A set of curtains
Pewter and earthenware.

Everything points to the fact that the marriage had been hasty and improvident—particularly the lack of a kettle. Equally, everything points to the fact that the youthful members of the household were light-hearted and content to share the chores. The household rather surprisingly included George Burnett, almost immediately after the wedding. The notebook indicates that the two young men got up at 6 o'clock and cleaned the kitchen, lit the fires, put on the 'tea-kettle', cleaned 'the insides of the boiling pot' and cleaned the shoes before Sara got the breakfast at 8 o'clock. It was the men who put the meat on the spit for dinner while Sara prepared the vegetables, and they lent her a hand with washing the dishes.

Coleridge's letters to Poole, Southey and Cottle rhapsodised over his marriage and his young wife with whom he now felt com-pletely in love. He wrote that he 'loved and was beloved, therefore happy'. He was married to the woman he 'loved best of all human kind'. And just after his wedding he wrote to Poole in a kind of fond ecstasy, reiterating 'Mrs Coleridge! Mrs Coleridge!—think of it!'

His Clevedon poems are shot with love and admiration for Sara, his 'sweet girl' which, taken in conjunction with his delight in their rose-twined cottage, makes their early days of marriage seem idyllic. As a symbol of romantic love the pair hung in their case-ment an Eolian harp, a simple frame or box with a few strings from which the breeze drew faint music. A wealthy Bristol trades-man looked over their garden-gate one Sunday and enviously remarked that their cottage was a blessed place. They agreed, and thought themselves blessed as well. Or did the poet invent this Bristol visitor?

Coleridge wrote, dug his small garden, and walked. It does not seem that Sara walked with him any more than at Nether Stowey. Sometimes he walked along the shore where black seaweed strewed the dark mud beyond the shingle at low tide. When he walked in the direction of Portishead he saw men gathering samphire below the craggy yellow cliffs one of which he described in his notebook as hanging over to 'glass' a rugged forehead in the calm sea. He lay on the slope of green Wain's Hill at noon to watch the sunlight strike diamonds from the sea's surface; he climbed Church Hill beyond St Andrew's Church that stands high between two hills, and he climbed steep and stony Dial Hill behind his cottage. He found each hill a magnificent look-out as we do today; but where we see the massed houses of the newer Clevedon that developed far in the opposite direction from the old church, he saw green hills, green fields, trees, corn, beanfields. However, if we walk the long steadily climbing cliff path between the shoulder of Wain's Hill and the sea—the sea lies on the right far below the steep fall of the yellow cliffs that in places are clouded with blue scabious in summertime—we walk where Coleridge certainly walked and see the landscape and seascape of which details are condensed in the Clevedon poems. Today of course, there are important additional details; sea-defences, a long sturdy sea-wall; clyses and floodgates constructed by the Somerset River Authority to control flooding of the great alluvial plain called Kenn Level that has been drained. Looking down on these one sees the little river Land Yeo that runs through lower Clevedon full of green reflections, to enter long, snake-like Clevedon Pill, the creek that in Coleridge's time was busy with craft and that now, in summer, contains tiny coloured pleasure-boats.

If the eye follows along the coastline it takes in jagged cliffs and a series of jutting headlands, including Brean Down, of which the wild, irregular line reaches back through summer haze or autumn mist to the 'heads' of the Quantocks and farther. Flat Holm and Steep Holm seemingly float on the water that on a calm day looks like a sheet of rippled grey silk unfolded to the Welsh coast. Coleridge, looking towards the Holms, saw the water dotted with white sails, as he mentions. He wrote nothing to indicate that he had seen the high tides battering these cliffs:

his 'Dim coasts and cloud-like hills and shoreless Ocean' suggest calm weather. With a certain amount of exaggeration he wrote in a letter that he had 'a prospect second to none in the kingdom'.

When he refers to a bare bleak mount speckled with sheep, from which he saw a faint city-spire, he meant Dial Hill from whose summit he could see Bristol spires as well as several village church-towers. One of the 'seats' was Clevedon Court, home of the Elton family, a beautiful house at East Clevedon now open to the public. As for the abbey, included in his view from a hill-top, it may have been the tower of ruined Woodspring Priory near Weston-super-Mare.

The first time he climbed one of these hills and looked at the prospect he declared that he had not a single thing to wish for. To *be* was enough. (He had forgotten his pantisocratic project.)

Yet he needed to keep his feet on the ground. He worked intermittently at his volume for Cottle and wrote a long religious poem 'The Nativity' or 'Religious Musings'. In November he preached his first sermon at the Unitarian Chapel in Bath, dressed in a white waistcoat and blue coat. Walking fifteen miles each way, he went to Bristol to use the public library and to meet friends at the Rummer Tavern with a view to organising a new periodical, part political, part literary, to be called *The Watchman*. In December he and Sara paid a visit to Tom Poole. By the end of the year Clevedon and love in a rose-bowered cottage had palled. He might set down some high-sounding reason for wanting to leave his honeymoon house, as in 'Reflections on Leaving a Place of Retirement' (written by the end of the year)—inability to idle his time happily away in flowery solitude while others 'toiled and bled'. He might tell Cottle that the distance from Bristol made it difficult to keep literary engagements and to supervise the printing of his poems, and that Sara was lonely in Clevedon with prying neighbours they disliked; all this was true. But the main reason for wanting to leave Clevedon for good was the boredom of living in a solitary place with no other company than Sara's.

Early in 1796 they moved to Bristol. They had to live at Mrs Fricker's on Redcliffe Hill where Coleridge felt cooped up as well as pressed for money. He had about 400 subscriptions promised for the forthcoming *Watchman*—not enough, so that he went off on a tour of the North and Midlands to collect more. His wife was pregnant and ailing. The tour in most ways was a brilliant triumph. Coleridge's sparkling eloquence astonished everyone he met, although everyone soon found that conversation always had to be one-sided. On several occasions he preached in Unitarian churches. He returned laden with subscriptions for his review—but endless troubles awaited him in Bristol, cares and vexations that he was not the man to cope with. Whenever he could escape he journeyed to Stowey to see Tom Poole who sent a quiet horse for him to ride—he disliked riding—from Bridgwater. At Stowey he sat in the arbour constructed from strips of oak-bark, under the big lime and not far from the reeking tan-pits. Here he recited his poems to Poole and talked of a hundred things in enthusiastic conversations that continued late into the night in the big parlour while they drank Stowey cider or Taunton ale: they talked of poetry, books, poets, of politics and of the social injustices that angered them both; of the new democratic ideas and ideals that had sprung from France before she was racked by the Terror; of his new review *The Watchman*, first published that March, price 4d. For Coleridge, a not inconsiderable advantage was the food prepared by old Mrs Poole and her servants in the Castle Street kitchen. During a fortnight's visit in May he ate honey-pie that he remembered when he wrote to Poole as he sat waiting early in the morning of 29 May for the Bristol coach from the George in Bridgwater. Poole was going through a phase when, like a number of abolitionists, he insisted on the use of honey, instead of sugar, in his household's pies, puddings and cakes.

His friendship with Poole was then the brightest spot in his existence. He was cheered because Poole's doctor brother, Richard, had written from Sherborne that he was keen to take the *Watchman* and that his *Poems*, published in April enchanted him. The other Pooles liked him no better than before. One April day Charlotte had gone to tea with her 'Aunt Thomas' in Castle Street. 'In the evening who should arrive but the famous Mr Coldridge', she wrote sarcastically in her journal, following this statement with her opinion that he was clever and extremely vain about it. During the May visit he had to break the news to Poole that his review *The Watchman* had utterly failed, leaving him £5 in debt after all his trouble. George Burnett, who supposedly helped him, had proved a broken reed, forgetting to send out copies to subscribers, sending in articles so badly written that Coleridge had to write them all over again. As for the *Poems*, they earned him little money and hardly any appreciation.

At this point Poole became his saviour. He wrote to half-a-dozen of Coleridge's friends who admired his work and believed that in time he would accomplish something outstanding. He proposed, and they agreed, to form a fund to which they would each contribute £5 annually so that Coleridge received about £40. The first £40 reached Coleridge from Mr Estlin, the treasurer, the day *The Watchman* failed. At least he was not destitute. His affection for Poole swelled his heart. From then on he regarded Poole as a port in many a storm. The words Poole wrote in the following year held good for Coleridge's lifetime. 'By you, Coleridge, I will always stand, in sickness and health, prosperity and misfortunes.'

But in spite of Poole's help his worries almost overwhelmed him as soon as he reached Bristol. He had to maintain George Burnett, himself, Sara, Mrs Fricker, a young Fricker boy: 'five mouths opening and shutting'. In a few months the child would be born; Sara wanted to buy baby-clothes and other necessities, was tearful and frightened about their future. He had secured only a small amount of reviewing and must search desperately for 'shilling-scavenger' employments. The stress under which he laboured brought on neuralgia; he began to dose himself with laudanum.

He departed to the Midlands again, wondering whether he should start a school.

THE ADSCOMBE PROJECT

While Coleridge was visiting Mr Lloyd the Birmingham banker in September 1796 a letter from Mr Maurice, Mrs Coleridge's medical attendant, informed him that a son had been born with no fuss whatever. This message sent him rushing home to Bristol and, with the usual lack of consideration he showed for his wife where domestic arrangements were concerned, he took Mr Lloyd's son Charles with him. Charles Lloyd possessed a small talent for poetry that Coleridge over-estimated and a character that Coleridge at that time admired, but he was handicapped by epilepsy. Both Charles and his father rejoiced that a man of Coleridge's brilliant intellect should accept him as boarder and pupil, while Coleridge felt that the small weekly sum he meant to ask would ease his own financial situation. Five days after the birth of Hartley, the son he would always love so intensely, Coleridge sat down to communicate all this news to Tom Poole and to ask if he might bring Charles Lloyd on a visit to Stowey where they could share a bed just as they did in the full Bristol household. Good-natured Poole welcomed them both and invited his neighbour young John Cruickshank to join them as they drank beer in the parlour looking out on Castle Street. Coleridge had of course already met John Cruickshank during an earlier visit and knew his wife Anna who was expecting a baby in December. The warm-hearted entertainment at Nether Stowey, the autumn-coloured landscape and laden orchards lying under the September sun, encouraged the already germinating idea in his mind that he would settle in this country district and divide his time between manual labour and 'literary occupation'. It encouraged also the fallacious belief—he outgrew it during the eighteen months in Nether Stowey—that country people led a life of innocence and rustic simplicity which would benefit the bodies and minds of his children. Accordingly he asked John Cruickshank whether in his capacity of agent to the Earl of Egmont, one of the most important local landowners, he could find him a small house. Cruickshank thought he could get him a house at Adscombe and Coleridge believed the matter as good as clinched. He wrote to Mr Lloyd telling him that he had thrown over all other schemes and that Charles Lloyd could live with the Coleridges in a cottage with 6 acres of land set in an enchanting situation 8 miles from Bridgwater and not very far from a dear friend of Coleridge's who would act as adviser in all matters.

No doubt he had walked with Cruickshank to Adscombe on a fine autumn afternoon, taking the road past Marshmills, past the mill and through a little maze of high-banked lanes rich in berries and late honeysuckle until they came upon the tiny hamlet that is part of Over Stowey parish. It was made up of Adscombe Farm and no more than four cottages and is not very much bigger today. Its situation deserved and still deserves Coleridge's adjective 'enchanting'. Not far from Adscombe Farm lay the opening to Seven Wells Combe, one of the most beautiful Quantock valleys, which was musical with the sound of running streams on which, in spring, the wild cherry and blackthorn dropped their petals. When Coleridge saw Seven Wells Wood in 1796 the first fiery colours of autumn had touched the oaks and beeches. A red earth track wound up through the yellowing bracken to Ramscombe and up higher to the heather-covered moorland plateau where the people of Over Stowey and Nether Stowey enjoyed commoners' rights of pasture. The present century has lessened the beauty with felling the oaks and beeches, with conifer planting, and with laying a road in Ramscombe.

Coleridge set his heart on living in this place from the moment he, Lloyd, and John Cruickshank, returned from their climb up Ramscombe, stood looking upward from Seven Wells Combe, dim with the first evening shadows, at the trees 'tinged yellow with the rich departing light'. Already he envisaged living in this 'woody dale' with his blue-eyed Sara who would greet him with a husband's kiss and Lloyd with a brother's. That evening he wrote for Charles Lloyd his poem, 'To a Young Friend On his proposing to domesticate with the Author'. He believed that within a few weeks they would be settled in a house at Adscombe and that John Cruickshank would arrange the tenancy.

It is hardly likely that he contemplated renting Adscombe Farm. The dwelling Cruickshank showed him may have been one of a pair of still-existing oak-beamed cottages or one of the pair called Chapel Cottages that were demolished at the end of the nineteenth century. These were built of stone taken from ruined Adscombe Chapel, and very old inhabitants say that the figures 1519 had been cut into the stonework. This date must have been cut before the chapel was abandoned.

Coleridge certainly saw ruined Adscombe Chapel on his little tour that September day, and many a time during later walks. Its last remains were pulled down, unexpectedly and regrettably, in 1964. The broken grey stonework of the west door archway and the ruined window, thickly wreathed in ivy, made a familiar landmark for many walkers although others never noticed it as its site on a little turf-platform cut into the side of a sloping field was not very conspicuous. It was all that the centuries had left of the chapel that belonged to the Abbey of Athelney.

During that same visit Tom Poole tentatively pointed out to him a very small, dark, thatched, unprepossessing cottage opening on to Lime Street in Nether Stowey. This, Poole thought, might soon be available, but he could not honestly recommend it as comfortable accommodation. He was not surprised when Coleridge waved aside the suggestion.

On 1 November Coleridge sent a very anxious letter to Poole as he had received no news from John Cruickshank. Had Cruickshank forgotten him, or had 'Lord Thing-a-my-Bob' refused to consider Coleridge as tenant? A few days later he wrote again. His anxiety about the Adscombe cottage had brought on an agonising attack of neuralgia in his face that had driven him nearly frantic. He was keeping it under with doses of laudanum and had a hot poultice under his ear. If the Adscombe cottage was not ready he must take temporary lodgings near Stowey for the winter. Couldn't William Poole let the Coleridges three rooms in his big house, Shurton Court? Coleridge hoped Tom Poole could arrange this without giving offence to William Poole. He hoped too that Tom Poole could find them a young servant.

Two days later another letter, rather contrite this time, went to Poole. Coleridge had heard from Cruickshank although nothing definite about Adscombe had been arranged. Cruickshank had explained that he was full of anxiety about his delicate wife Anna and her approaching confinement. Coleridge's own anxiety made him write two more letters to Poole in the following week and haunt the Bristol post office every evening for the reply which never came until the 28th. This time he eagerly fell in with Poole's suggestion that he should temporarily rent the cottage in Lime Street even if no one could call it 'a beauty'. He told Poole to take it for a year. They *must* be out of their Bristol home by Christmas. He wrote next to Mr Lloyd to inform him that Charles could board with him at Stowey for half a guinea weekly if he paid for his own washing and any alcoholic drink more potent than beer, and if he furnished his own room. He no longer thought he could act as Charles' tutor as his days would be filled with husbandry and his evenings with writing for reviews. He wrote a gay letter to Poole although he did not yet feel quite assured that 'the little cottage by the roadside' was 'gettable', and told Poole how hard he meant to work at a dozen occupations when installed there.

By mid-December Coleridge was bombarding Poole with frantic, nearly hysterical letters; his plans seemed crashing round his head; he was indescribably harassed about money matters and about finding a home for his wife and child by Christmas. Sara continually worried him with apprehensive questions. Poole, it was plain, had had second thoughts. His doubts that the Lime Street cottage would suit the Coleridges lingered and he thought Coleridge would do better to settle at Iron Acton, near Bristol. Coleridge would save himself 3 guineas by not moving to Stowey.

Why this change of heart, Coleridge demanded. Had old Mrs Poole objected to having the Coleridges live near? What friends would he have at Acton where the scenery was flat as Holland and hateful to him? If Cruickshank could not buy the Adscombe cottage and repair it—as he had promised—some Birmingham friends of Coleridge probably would. And while he waited for it, the Lime Streeet cottage would *do* after Coleridge had altered the fireplace and excluded draughts; he would *make* it do, he wrote, underlining his words, in fact three rooms would suffice. He gave Poole full domestic and financial details. He earned 40 guineas a year reviewing and could earn more. If he cut down on meat-eating, Mrs Coleridge could keep them and their child on 16s a week (she had worked it out herself) as long as he grew their vegetables and kept a pig. He relied on Poole to teach him the management of his 1½ acre domain.

He wrote again next day to repeat that Poole's hesitation had chilled his heart as well as adding to his intolerable burdens. They would do without a servant and put out the washing to a Stowey washerwoman. Sara could concentrate on sewing and look-ing after the child if he helped her with the housework. Even *two* rooms would do. His volume of poems for Cottle was ready so that he had no pressing literary work on hand; in fact he rashly promised 'that Literature will always be a secondary Object with me'. All he desired was to live near Poole in that tiny cottage and to work hard to support his family. Poole's company would compensate for every disadvantage.

'I adhere to Stowey,' wrote Coleridge, 'unless circumstances have lessened your love or esteem.'

CHAPTER 4

THE COTTAGE IN LIME STREET

'Nether Stowey—sanctum et amabile nomen!'—S. T. Coleridge

Nine days before Christmas 1796 Tom Poole yielded to Coleridge's anguished appeals and acquired for him the tenancy of the thatched cottage in Lime Street called Gilbards. The rent was eight guineas a year, payable quarterly, and Coleridge became the sub-tenant of the widowed Elizabeth Rendle whose husband had rented it from the owner Robert Blake until 1794.

After receiving Poole's letter Coleridge sat down on the Saturday night to write to John Thelwall whom he had long neglected. He told Thelwall that at Stowey he would cultivate a garden of 1½ acres, raising corn and vegetables for his household and feeding two pigs on the refuse. The rest of his time would be divided between composing his poetry, reading, and writing reviews for magazines or carrying out other 'shilling-scavenger employments' which must produce £40 per year, an amount he thought he could make economy hammer out, like a gold beater, to cover all his family expenses. Three weeks later he wrote triumphantly and gaily to Thelwall that he was carrying out his programme. He was growing potatoes and all sorts of vegetables and proposed to raise corn with the spade. He had an orchard. In addition to the pigs he kept ducks and geese. There was no need to keep a cow as he obtained all their milk from Tom Poole. He gardened from seven till half past eight; read and composed till noon, then looked after his livestock until two o'clock dinner; worked again till tea, did his reviewing till supper time.

He did not mention to Thelwall the omnivorous reading that

so often occupied him until after midnight, when his chatty wife and lively baby son were asleep and his was the only lighted candle pricking the darkness of Lime Street. 'The light shall stream to a far distance from the taper in my cottage window', he wrote to Thelwall in his December letter, a statement more truly prophetic than he ever guessed. But the eagerness to cultivate his piece of land soon waned. Not without reason did twenty-two year old Charles Lamb remark 'And pray what does your worship know about farming?'

On Sunday morning 18 December Coleridge had written a swift reply to Poole, fervently grateful, and very apologetic for his recent hysterical reproaches. As his face was swollen with neuralgia, his apothecary would not let him carry out his economical plan of walking the 42 miles from Bristol to Stowey. However he meant to get to Stowey by mid-week, ahead of the goods waggon and at least a week ahead of Sara. He thought of hiring a waggon privately to take his chattels direct to Stowey; this might be cheaper than loading them on drays to be carried to the public waggon from Bristol to Bridgwater where they must be repacked on a vehicle for Stowey. No, they would certainly not want any of the woman's (Mrs Rendle's) furniture as they had chests of drawers, kitchen furniture, chairs, one bed and bed linen, not to mention Coleridge's boxes of books. Coleridge would bring a dozen yards of the cheap material called green list, for plugging draughts which he abominated. If there was a fireplace one of the chimneys might be Rumfordised. Coleridge had recently reviewed Count Rumford's *Essays* and had a craze for 'Rumfordising'.

In the end, Coleridge had to remain three days longer in Bristol, having tardily remembered that he had promised a newspaper editor some lines for the last day of the year. He managed to finish them over Christmas, went to bed for two days with a feverish cold, wrote several reviews in a rush, and finally arrived in Nether Stowey with Sara and the baby, on Saturday the last day of 1796. No doubt Tom Poole sent his chaise into Bridgwater for them.

During the early weeks of the new year Coleridge was immensely happy. His letters of that period sparkle with a happiness undimmed by his continual carking poverty, and his poor, cramped, inconvenient dwelling. Never again were he and Sara to enjoy such domestic felicity. He was only twenty-four, extremely fond of his young wife if never passionately in love with her. They would come out of Poole's house on a starry night and walk home with his arm around her. She was a devoted mother to Hartley, and Coleridge himself adored this beautiful child to whom he wrote the lines 'A little child, a limber elf', and for whom, more prosaically, he endured sitting with a napkin pinned on his knee to warm by the fire while he was writing a poem. When Richard Reynell, a friend who at that time thought of boarding with Coleridge, visited the cottage in August, he declared that it was a treat to see Coleridge hanging over his infant and talking to him. The child was 'a noble, healthy-looking fellow, strong eyebrows, beautiful eyes'. As for Sara Coleridge, Reynell praised her highly: sensible, affable, good-natured, thrifty, industrious, always neat and prettily dressed, 'indeed a pretty woman'. Furthermore Reynell found what to him seemed an idyllic domestic life, full of beauty and simplicity, where the poor cottage and lack of riches did not count. Yet only four years later Coleridge wrote that the great Matchmaker never brought together two minds 'so utterly contrariant' and that in his early married life he 'was often almost miserable'. And years after their sordid quarrels had led them to live in separate establishments, he reputedly confided to a friend that when they had a servantless period at Stowey Mrs Coleridge was cruel enough on a winter morning, when snow lay on the ground and icicles decked their cottage eaves, to compel him to get out of bed in his nightshirt and light the fire before she would consent to dress herself and the baby. Nevertheless, none of the letters he wrote from Stowey before the autumn of 1798 reveal any such discord.

Apart from happiness in his marriage, Coleridge was lit by another flame. During those eighteen months at Stowey he wrote every one of his greatest poems, almost all of them at the Lime Street cottage. The last twelve months made his 'Annus Mirabilis' when, in closest contact with the Wordsworths and with the landscape of the Quantocks and west Somerset, he seemed—to quote his biographer Professor Chambers—to walk in company with some daimon or genius. This flame of poetic achievement burned itself out with dazzling swiftness during that single twelve-month. From Germany in 1799 he wrote to Poole, 'My Muse is quite gone. Perhaps she may return and meet me at Stowey'. This hope was never realised.

For Mrs Coleridge the writing of poetry was only a means of earning an income, and a highly unsatisfactory one. She grew to like Stowey very much, but in later days always referred to their Lime Street home as a miserable cottage. Indeed, from the first days its defects must have hit her hard and have led to frequent complaining. It had three poky bedrooms with low ceilings and sloping floors. Maybe a partition made the three bedrooms into four because, when Reynell came, one bedroom had for its window only a pane of glass made to slide in and out by means of a piece of wire. Downstairs there was a small dark parlour on each side of the front door, and at the back a very primitive kitchen with cold flagged floor and a fire on the hearth without any oven. Over this fire Sara had to heat water for a big monthly washday such as she was coping with when John Thelwall turned up. When she wanted to provide a roast, the joint had to be carried to the Stowey bake-house like the leg of pork and baked potatoes that Coleridge, in jovial verse written on the back of a lecture-prospectus, invited Tom Poole to dine on one day in January. The chimney of one parlour-grate smoked abominably and at times gave Coleridge an excuse for escaping to Alfoxden because the fumes set up inflammation in his eyes. And mice ran about unchecked because Coleridge pretended that it irked him to invite them hypocritically into a trap by offering a bait of toasted cheese.

In February the cramped accommodation of the cottage was further strained by the arrival of young Charles Lloyd as Coleridge's boarder, and as the Coleridges could not afford to furnish another room Lloyd bought a press-bed that enabled him to use his bedroom as a sitting-room. In March his frequent epileptic fits entailed on Coleridge the additional burden of nursing and caused many broken nights.

Another bedroom was occupied by Nanny, the young servant-girl. Possibly Poole found the situation for her as in November Coleridge had asked him to look out for a suitable maid, a nice-looking one if possible. Nanny went away to Bristol with Mrs

Coleridge in 1799 and for some reason never came back to Stowey, but the Coleridges always spoke of her with much affection. 'Be sure to give my kind love to Nanny' was a message in one of Coleridge's letters from Germany, and a few weeks after the death of his baby son Berkeley, he wrote to his wife, 'It grieves me to the heart that Nanny is not with you'. He always remembered how much Nanny had loved the firstborn Hartley and how she had been at pains to teach the intelligent lively child some of his first words and tricks, yet if one can accept as reliable the gossip picked up by De Quincey ten years later, Nanny was the servant who told Stowey people how much she pitied poor Mrs Coleridge on account of her husband's open preference for the company of Dorothy Wordsworth, and for having to put up with Dorothy Wordsworth's thoughtless behaviour. Nanny allegedly told a story of how Dorothy, with William and Coleridge, came back to the cottage for supper after a day's walking on the hills, Dorothy draggled like a gipsy and taking the liberty of running up to the Coleridges' bedroom and helping herself 'with much merriment' to a dress from the Coleridges' cupboard to wear while her own dried.

As a hostess Sara Coleridge must have found it difficult to find sleeping accommodation for the visitors Coleridge invited for a stay. Cottle, Hazlitt, George Burnett from Huntspill, Richard Reynell from Devon, Charles Lamb, Charles Lloyd after he had finished living with them, were among the guests who spent a couple of nights or even three weeks under the cottage roof. By late spring, Lloyd had departed, but even so she must have been obliged to seek help from Tom Poole's mother—either a bedroom or some bedding—when in July she had to entertain Charles Lamb for a week just when Coleridge had brought the Wordsworths from Racedown to spend a fortnight looking round the district for a house. Preparing meals for so many people in her primitive kitchen made her so flustered that she tipped a pan of scalding milk over Coleridge's foot, which deprived him of walking the hills with Lamb and the Wordsworths. Yet other visitors besides Richard Reynell found Sara a cheerful and competent hostess who made them welcome. Joseph Cottle thought that Coleridge with his pretty wife holding the baby in her arms made a picture of

Page 89 This house was formerly the Globe Inn, Castle, Nether Stowey. The government agent stayed here in 1797 when investigating the 'spy' rumours

Page 90 Castle Inn, Bridgwater, near the bridge. The photograph was taken in about 1880 and the inn has since been demolished. De Quincey probably came here in 1807 domestic bliss out in the summer garden. Charles Lamb wrote to Coleridge that Coleridge's dear Sara had become very dear to him also, 'because so very kind'. He also apologised for having appeared unsociable and sullen in the midst of a gathering of Coleridge's friends at Cruickshank's cottage; he had got out of the habit of making gay conversation. Poor Lamb! He was only twenty-two but the black shadow of his mother's death at the hands of his deranged sister lay across his existence. Finally, he asked whether any waggon from Stowey could bring his forgotten greatcoat part of the journey to London, and he was still writing to Stowey about it months later when winter was approaching, telling Coleridge that all he had was 'a wretched old coat' of his father's.

So content was Coleridge with his new life at the cottage, even in the depths of January, that he gaily advised John Thelwall—he wrote with the first callouses of his early gardening efforts on his palms—to try a similar existence. Many features of his cheaply rented dwelling gave him pleasure. A clear brook of very soft water babbled past his front door, the brook that worked the mill in the neighbouring lane where the old sluices remain. In the back yard a well with a windlass supplied fresh drinking water from a spring. Their garden was both useful and pretty, and they had 'a sweet orchard' as well. One moonlight night when little Hartley woke crying, Coleridge carried him into the orchard and showed him the full moon. Tom Poole had set a gate in the hedge dividing this orchard from his own garden so that the Coleridges could make their way easily into Poole's garden and through the tanyard into Poole's house, or alternatively go through Poole's own orchard and across a meadow into John Cruickshank's garden. Cruickshank is supposed to have been tenant of the present Ivy Cottage. When Cottle came later in the summer, Coleridge proudly took him round the premises, showing him his house, his garden, his fruit-laden orchard and the 'contrivances' he had made to unite his two neighbours' domains with his own. 'Mr C. took particular delight in assuring me, at least at that time, how happy he was,' Cottle recollected. At the end of their little tour they sat down with Tom Poole and Charles Lloyd in Poole's rustic arbour, under

F

the spreading, fragrant lime with the birds singing in the tree and the sunlight falling dappled through its leaves. Here bread-and-cheese and mugs of Taunton ale were set out on a three-legged table, and as they feasted, laughed and talked, every interstice of their hearts, in Cottle's words, was filled with happiness. They were all of them young. Wordsworth himself recorded that Coleridge in his gayest mood was as noisy and gamesome as a boy, tossing his limbs in sheer delight like tree-branches in the wind. His golden eloquence, his unwearying capacity to talk, his power to hold a listener as spellbound as the Wedding Guest of his own creation, became legendary as well as, at times, the subject for jest among his friends. However, Cornelia Crosse, the second wife of Andrew Crosse of Broomfield, recorded in her reminiscences, *Red Letter Days*, that the aged mother of a friend had met Coleridge and found him 'an absentminded, opinionated man, talking everybody down, fatiguing to listen to'.

The Coleridges found no lack of daily company. 'I have society, my *friend* T. Poole and as many acquaintances as I can dispense with,' wrote Coleridge. At first, like most newcomers, he got invited to local social gatherings where he met a number of pretty young women fond of music, dancing and conversation. His lively talk, his puns and conundrums, amused them highly; he even deigned to listen to their own chatter. They started teaching him to dance, a new accomplishment for Coleridge. When Coleridge wrote home from Germany about dancing, Mrs Coleridge expressed prim disapproval. The invitations to Stowey parties did not continue very long.

John Cruickshank became a fairly intimate friend who came frequently to the cottage and sometimes accompanied Coleridge to Alfoxden. After the Wordsworths arrived, however, their companionship sufficed Coleridge without any other except Poole's but he kept up a few lesser friendships. He was friendly with William Roskilly the Cornish curate who kept a boarding-school, charging £20 per annum to include washing and Latin. From Germany he wrote Roskilly a gay congratulatory letter when Roskilly had obtained the living of Kempsford. He may even have gone along to church with Sara on 3 February to witness the baptism by Mr Roskilly of Cruickshank's baby Anna Elizabeth.

The verses he wrote afterwards 'On the Christening of a Friend's Child' were a tribute mainly to her mother whom Coleridge admired for the pure goodness of her character from the day he met her as Anna Buckle of Enmore where she married John Cruickshank on 3 October 1795, the day before Coleridge's own wedding. John was the eldest son—Coleridge's age—of William Cruickshank, agent to the Earl of Egmont's Enmore estate, and in 1793 had been admitted to Middle Temple. He became a subscriber to the £40 fund organised for Coleridge but the suggestion that he should be treasurer was turned down on account of his recklessness about money that afterwards landed him in serious trouble. In later years Coleridge wrote that his heart ached for 'poor Cruickshank's distresses', but Mrs Coleridge made priggish comments on the extravagance of these former friends, writing to Poole in 1818 that she was *not* quite sure whether she 'sympathised with their embarrassments' as she 'suspected great mismanagement'. Cruickshank left Stowey in 1799 soon after the summer day when he drove Southey in his chaise to Porlock.

One thing Coleridge never forgot. Cruickshank told him, one morning in 1797, that he had had a curious dream about a skeleton ship manned by ghostly figures. The memory of Cruickshank's dream swam to the surface of consciousness as Coleridge walked with the Wordsworths to Watchet in waning November daylight.

Cruickshank introduced Coleridge to the Earl of Egmont, Baron Lovel and Holland of Enmore, and to his sister Lady Elizabeth Perceval. The earl had served under Ferdinand of Brunswick, been Lord Lieutenant of Somerset and Tory MP for Bridgwater, yet his views were sufficiently liberal for him to be friendly with Fox and John Chubb whose portraits of him show an aristocratic face of great distinction. He was brother of the Prime Minister Perceval who was later assassinated and to whom Coleridge once thought of applying, through the earl, for a post in Africa. Without greatly appreciating poetry Lord Egmont gave Coleridge considerable encouragement and at times hospitality.

A friend introduced by Poole was the merchant John Chubb whose warehouse near the Dolphin Inn, (which was demolished a few years ago like the last stones of Chubb's house and where Coleridge *could* have seen the prototype of his Ancient Mariner),

looked on Back Quay (now Binford Place) by the Parret. Chubb
had been Mayor of Bridgwater, was a close friend of Charles
James Fox, and held extremely liberal opinions although he had
the sense to decline helping Coleridge to install the revolutionary John Thelwall in a house near Stowey. From time to
time he gave the Coleridges generous hospitality. He was a cultured man who loved music and the arts, gave celebrated glee-
parties and spent hours sitting in fields and streets on a camp-
stool making water-colour sketches of Bridgwater subjects that
still give delight and reveal considerable talent. It is a great pity
that his portraits of various friends and local personalities did
not include one of Coleridge. His young son Morley went to Mr
Roskilly's boarding-school.

Coleridge counted the two elderly ministers Mr Howel and Dr
Toulmin as friends. By the autumn of 1797 he was on the verge
of entering the Unitarian ministry himself, impelled mainly by
financial reasons although he took no payment from Mr Howel
and Dr Toulmin. As in Bristol and Bath he generally wore a blue
coat and white waistcoat when he preached; this costume in conjunction with his tumbling black hair and fiery oratory made him
a figure in striking contrast to the usual sober, black-clad minister.
Stories of his preaching ability got around so that on at least one
occasion in Bridgwater members 'of all the best families in the
town' attended the chapel in Dampiet Street. A few members of
his congregations criticised his uncombed hair. He must have
looked dusty and travel-stained for he always walked on these
journeys, using lonely lanes on his way to Bridgwater and the
rough, red-banked by-roads skirting Aisholt and winding through
Spaxton and Charlynch. He climbed up the Quantock ridge and
walked along part of the prehistoric packway before dropping
down the wooded slope to Kingston St Mary or Cothelstone to
reach Taunton. Perhaps his blue coat needed mending that July
day he sent a note round to Tom Poole by Nanny asking if she
could bring back a coat Poole had said he might have. 'I wish to
have it made fit for me for next Sunday.'

He remained friendly with young George Burnett who would
walk over from Huntspill to Stowey for a day or longer. Once
when Coleridge was on his way back from Bristol he called at

Burnett's home and found him horribly ill with jaundice. 'I wish my pockets were as yellow as George's phiz!' he wrote, thinking ruefully of the guineas that so seldom came his way. By April monetary worries had begun to cloud his happiness and that same month he began to realise that his political opinions were rousing local hostility. This came home to him when, during a journey from Bristol, a woman asked him if he knew a fellow from Bristol called Coleridge whose revolutionary opinions had exercised an evil influence over young Burnett from her own parish. 'A vile Jacobin villain' she called him. Coleridge expressed horror and left the woman thinking him a nice young gentleman.

He greatly liked John Chester of Nether Stowey who joined him and Hazlitt on their walk to Lynton but Chester, several years his senior, was the open-mouthed admirer, never a friend on equal terms. Coleridge's attitude towards Chester was one of good-natured tolerance.

Both Coleridge and Sara were very fond of Poole's bright-faced apprentice, 'little Tommy Ward' and, when away from Stowey, never wrote to Poole without sending their love and remembrances to Ward. Mrs Coleridge kept up the habit for thirty years. Often Ward was unobtrusively present when Coleridge came to sit and talk to Poole in the parlour. Like many others he listened to Coleridge's talk with the utmost admiration and took pleasure in performing tasks and errands for him. When Poole's clerk Richard Govett mended a batch of quill pens for Coleridge, Ward, afraid they were not good enough, made another consignment and sent them round to the cottage. By return came one of Coleridge's sparkling, punning letters to his 'pennefactor' 'composed' wrote Coleridge, 'in Apollo's Temple in the odoriferous Lime-Grove, alias Street'. Perhaps this was an early sarcastic criticism of the house that got whiffs from the tanyard and not from lime trees that October day.

At times Coleridge suggested in a letter to Tom Poole from Germany or London that Ward might do this or that; Ward could run round to the shut-up cottage and look for a book on Godwin left on a shelf in the parlour; Ward could take it into Bridgwater and put it on the Exeter coach; Ward could find a box of books left by Coleridge in a small room upstairs at Poole's; Ward could make copies of the long letters he sent from Germany in case his descriptions of the Harz mountains and other places came in useful. All these jobs young Ward carried out with eager willingness. He could not foresee how grateful posterity would be for those transcriptions of Coleridge's letters. Several years later it was Ward's brother, a London bookseller, who undertook to receive the subscriptions paid for Coleridge's periodical, *The Friend*.

The lives of humbler people could touch his sympathy. A poor Stowey man known as old Daddy Rich and his wife lived nearby, in the utmost terror of their crazy son. When the cry of 'Murder!' reached Coleridge's ears one day, he rushed out to rescue old Rich from his son's cruel beating. The lunatic swore vengeance on Coleridge, even on the infant Hartley. Mrs Rich performed various domestic jobs for Mrs Coleridge when the latter was absent from Stowey. Mrs Coleridge would write a few lines from Bristol to Mrs Rich; she feared that the cottage was getting damp, would Mrs Rich please look in? She could open the cottage windows on a fine day. 'How is poor old Mr Rich and his wife?' enquired Coleridge when writing to Poole from Keswick in 1800. In spite of their tribulations the Riches attained a ripe old age. Twenty years later Mrs Coleridge wrote to Poole that she was glad to hear of poor Rich's release and to know that Mrs Rich had just enough to live on 'without labour'.

Rich, Cole, Knight, Waite, Virgin, Clitsome, Kibby, Criddle, Verrier, Sully, Day, Webber, Blake, these were among the Nether Stowey family names familiar to the Coleridges. Some exist in Stowey today, and those that have vanished could be found there a few years ago.

Coleridge thoroughly despised the Stowey doctor, or surgeon as he was styled. This is hardly surprising as Coleridge suffered greatly at his hands, being afflicted with unsound teeth that gave him a lot of trouble besides flawing his looks. When an aching stump began to suppurate he asked the surgeon to extract it. His unsuccessful struggle increased the pain to such a pitch that Coleridge declared he would sooner put his hands in a lion's mouth 'than put my mouth in his hands'. The intense pain gave him sleepless nights so that he resorted to doses of laudanum which brought him repose, but not sleep. (Laudanum was a pain-

killer in common use and Dorothy Wordsworth took it for tooth-
ache.) The Wordsworths invited him, and Sara too, for a week at
Alfoxden, where he rested and recuperated free of domestic worry.
From Alfoxden he wrote the refusal of an invitation to Bristol
informing his correspondent that Mrs Coleridge's second lying-in
was only a few weeks away and he felt that he could not leave her,
especially as her surgeon had inherited little skill from
Aesculapius. Besides, their house was an uncomfortable one. Perhaps the grace and space of Alfoxden had sharply brought home
the limitations of the cottage in Lime Street. However, they had
lived in Nether Stowey for fifteen months before Coleridge wrote
in this disparaging manner about his dwelling. As it turned out he
had no need to worry about Mrs Coleridge who gave birth to
Berkeley, their second son, at half-past one on a May morning. At
three o'clock that morning Coleridge wrote to Mr Estlin that she
had been delivered of a fine boy and that she had had 'a remarkably good time, better if possible than her last'. When Hartley
was born in Bristol she had delivered her baby herself quite
competently before the midwife or the doctor, Mr Maurice,
arrived. (And when Derwent was born at Keswick, in the year
following Coleridge's return from Germany, Coleridge wrote very
proudly that Sara was up and drinking tea with him in the
parlour on the third day.)

Mrs Coleridge would scarcely have been human if, pregnant
for the second time and tied down by a twelve-month toddler in
a comfortless cottage, she had not felt some resentment when
Coleridge spent the greater part of his days with the Wordsworths,
either at Alfoxden walking the hills or going on much longer
expeditions, or at the Lime Street cottage where she prepared
meals for everybody and often dried wet clothes. She was a fairly
intelligent, if commonplace, woman and could not have been blind
to the fact that Dorothy Wordsworth and Coleridge found harm-
ony and completeness in each other's company and that they spent
hours alone together, sometimes the one escorting the other from
Alfoxden or Stowey by moonlight or in darkness. Frequently she
must have felt excluded from the conversation of Coleridge and
the Wordsworths; where intellectual matters or the making of
poetry were concerned she was certainly odd man out and could

not understand why Samuel—Coleridge hated the name and everybody else called him Coleridge or Col—would not take a regularly paid situation, such as journalism or schoolmastering, which would relieve their perpetual shortage of money. They had no regular income (before January 1798) except the £40 fund administered by Mr Estlin, whereas the Wordsworths had no family to rear, possessed a modest annuity from the legacy Raisley Calvert had bequeathed William, and therefore could afford this odd, disorganised way of living. There is no evidence that Sara was ever incivil towards the Wordsworths although some years later, when Coleridge quoted various ways in which she had made their marriage fail, he said that she had often received his friends with freezing looks. But certainly she had little in common with William or Dorothy and when the Wordsworths moved to the Lake District was not enthusiastic about moving to be near them, while Coleridge's main reason for going to Keswick when he could not find another house in Stowey was the fact that the Wordsworths' company would be available. His secondary reason was the comforting knowledge that the move would take him further away from his Bristol in-laws.

When finally they did move Coleridge, with masculine self-deception, wrote that there were advantages for Sara as she had little society in Stowey. True, some months before they left, the widow of Tom Poole's brother Richard had come to live in Stowey with her new-born baby and had picked a quarrel with Mrs Coleridge, even turning her unpleasantness on little Hartley. And in a letter to Poole from Germany Coleridge remarked that really nobody in Nether Stowey liked them except Poole himself. Yet for the most part Sara Coleridge was well content in Stowey; in after years she frequently alluded to 'happy Stowey days', and to 'beloved Stowey' in her letters to Poole. While living in Lime Street she enjoyed the small social activities of a little town. She was very friendly with Mrs Roskilly, drank tea with her, admired her baby, Mary Elizabeth, born, like Hartley, in 1796. She ran in and out of the Cruickshanks' house by means of the orchard gate to gossip with sweet-natured little Anna Cruickshank. Their babies were about the same age and the two young mothers were 'extremely cordial', to quote Coleridge. She was friendly with the

Misses Brice whose father later became Vicar of Aisholt. Old
Mrs Poole was extremely fond of Sara and always ready to offer
help. On one occasion she gave her a forequarter of lamb that
made a celebration feast for the Wordsworths' arrival at Alfoxden.
A Mr and Mrs James Cole were among her friends and helped
her in a time of trouble when Coleridge was away. She knew the
mother and sisters of John Chester. It is quite likely, however,
that at times she missed the shops and the lively atmosphere of
her native Bristol, as well as her sisters' society.

The distance from Bristol had been one of the disadvantages
that Tom Poole pointed out to Coleridge who, as time went on,
soon found that Poole was not mistaken. Except for the collection
of books that Poole himself had built up he depended, for his
enormous and comprehensive reading, on the Bristol library to
which he was a subscriber. He read in depth, making notes in a
'commonplace book' or, if the book were his own, annotating the
pages. (Any book annotated by Coleridge is now a collector's
treasure.) Soon he was in trouble over keeping books too long,
with Mr Catcott the sub-librarian whose 'expensive little notes and
letters' on which, of course, Coleridge had to pay the postage,
cost him 5s, a sum he felt much too poor to afford. He gave himself the satisfaction of writing Mr Catcott a lofty letter, reminding him that he did not borrow light novels but 'books of massy
knowledge' and that even if the members of the library committee
were clever enough to read over 2,000 closely printed pages of
Greek and Latin in three weeks, he himself was no such genius.
Still, the difficulties and expense that so great a distance from a
library entailed on a reader who styled himself a library-cormorant
were undeniable.

The distance from Bristol involved him in greater trouble where
his own poetry was concerned. During his first busy week of
settling into the cottage he sent his publisher Cottle a painstaking
letter about the arrangement of his poems for the 1797 volume
as well as details of revisions for Biggs the printer. The twenty-
three main poems included 'The Beautiful Spring in a Village',
'Shurton Bars', 'Low was our pretty Cot'. This letter was written
on a Friday when some messenger took it to the post in Bridgwater, but the parcel of manuscript would not reach Cottle before

the following Thursday. It had to be transported by Milton, the Stowey carrier, who set out from Stowey every Wednesday, and it would have reached Cottle on the Thursday before the date of Coleridge's letter if the erratic Milton had not left Stowey two hours earlier than usual.

Milton the carrier, with his waggon and horses, made a link of communication between Nether Stowey and the outside world. Every Wednesday morning he jolted past the gazebo, court house and church onto the Bridgwater road, carrying letters, parcels, goods like cheeses and kegs of cider, as well as one or two passengers, and facing a journey of over forty miles. In Bridgwater he picked up any letters left at the Angel Inn, and left any he had collected en route for Bridgwater recipients. If commissioned to do so he sent letters by post from Bridgwater. Somewhere on the way to Bristol—probably at the village of Cross used by many travellers as a stopping-place—he slept a night in his waggon or over the inn stable, and on Thursday he finally delivered the rest of his cargo at the Bear Inn in Redcliffe Street, Bristol. A few hours later he started on the return journey with packets collected at the Bear, at Cottle's bookshop in Wine Street, Bristol, and at other places, so that his waggon rolled back into Stowey on Friday evening. He was somewhat sullen and disobliging, especially when in a hurry, and several times waited ungraciously when he found young Mr Coleridge still scribbling furiously at an unfinished letter in the smoky parlour. Not unnaturally he pressed him to hurry up or even went on his way. On the Wednesday morning in January 1797 when Coleridge wrote to Mr Estlin his rapturous description of the newly acquired cottage, he had to cut his letter short with the sentence ' I have 50 things to write but the carrier is at the Door'.

All that summer Milton carried letters from Lime Street: letters to Cottle, to Mr Estlin, to Southey; letters about the cottage and mounting bills; letters about the visit to Racedown and the Wordsworths' arrival at Alfoxden. On a mid-July morning when the air smelt of lime-blossom he picked up the letter for Southey that contained the first draft of the lovely poem 'This Lime Tree Bower My Prison'. Mr Coleridge hobbled on a bandaged foot as he came to the door. When the Lime Street cottage was shut,

Milton continued carrying correspondence between Stowey and Bristol on the Coleridges' behalf: Coleridge wrote to his wife via Tom Poole, perhaps to save on expensive postage from Germany, and Poole sent the letter with a kindly letter from himself, to Sara in Bristol by Milton who carried back from Sara a cargo of fears and complaints, her request for Mr Poole to lend her ten guineas, sometimes a sad query 'Is there no letter from Samuel?' and once a heartrending letter that began 'Oh my dear Mr Poole! I have lost my dear, dear child'.

The installation of the Wordsworths at Alfoxden in the height of summer 1797 brought Coleridge a golden happiness that irradiated the following twelve months and turned them, in spite of all his harassing cares, into the unique splendid year, shining and memorable, of his whole life so that he looked back on it and marvelled, often with deep melancholy. His joy in living and his powers of creation reached their apex within its span. Nevertheless the Wordsworths had hardly arrived when Coleridge found himself disagreeably involved in an affair that embittered him against the people of Nether Stowey and Holford. This affair was the Wordsworth spy scare (Chapter 7). Coleridge found himself followed on his walks. He noticed hostile stares, significant nods and nudges, sullen mutterings, among the local people, especially on occasions when he carried his memorandum book and pencilled notes in it during his wanderings. He had conceived the idea of writing a long philosophic poem on some subject that would give him 'room for description and incident as well as for impassioned reflection on men, nature, society'. The subject would be symbolic and would link the various parts of the poem into a unified whole. By the summer he had decided on the symbolic subject; the brook he followed frequently in the course of his walks, whether solitary or with the Wordsworths or alone with Dorothy, during those weeks of full summer. It was the Quantock stream that hurries over its pebbled bed through Butterfly Combe (sometimes called Tannery Combe) where today the picnic-parties park their cars on summer days at the broad open place under the swell of Danesborough, just below the spot where the stream runs out of a sullen, branch-overhung pool. Coleridge had traced it from where the first silver threads emerged at its source above

Holford for the whole length of its channel through the long
narrow combe, past the big water-wheel that can still be seen,
down to the wooded glen at Holford and over the fields to the
sea at Kilve. As he followed its windings he jotted an occasional
note or, as he put it, made studies, and when he passed a man
working in a field or walking behind a flock of sheep asked him
questions about this little water-course, sometimes in a facetious
tone as when he asked whether it were navigable. This was the
same stream that Dorothy Wordsworth mentioned in her journal
in the following year, saying that they had found its source.
Coleridge called his poem 'The Brook'. He wrote later:

> Such a subject I conceived myself to have found in a stream
> traced from its source in the hills among the yellow-red moss
> and conical glass-shaped tufts of bents to the 1st break or fall
> where its drops become audible and it begins to form a channel;
> thence to the peat and turf-barn itself built of the same dark
> squares it shelters, to the sheepfold, to the 1st cultivated plot
> of ground, to the lonely cottage and its bleak garden won from
> the heath; to the hamlet, the villages, the market-town, the
> manufactories, and the sea-port.

The poem itself was never written. Coleridge recorded that his
studies for it roused the suspicions of the local residents and the
government agent. Viewed over a gap of two centuries the episode
seems absurd, yet it was no more absurd than some that arose in
the last war when amateur photographers or watercolour-artists
in the same area as Coleridge, found themselves interrogated by
a policeman after a report by suspicious inhabitants. The fear of
French invasion was very strong and well-grounded. 'Expect the
French any dark night' said William Pitt. It was not surprising
that people living in remote places near the coast got nervous
about unusual activities. Coleridge did, however, leave one of his
'studies' for 'The Brook' in the *Gutch Memorandum Book*.

> The Brook runs over sea-weeds—
> Sabbath day—from the Miller's mossy wheel
> The waterdrops dripp'd leisurely—
> On the broad mountaintop
> The neighing wild-colt races with the wind

O'er fern and heath-flowers—
A long deep lane
So overshadowed it might seem one bower.
The damp clay banks were furr'd with mouldy moss,
Broad-breasted Pollards with broad-branching head.

Anyone familiar today with Butterfly Combe will recognise the description as perfect.

As a poet he was working, not only on the tragedy *Osorio* that Sheridan had commissioned. From his quickened observation, from buried memories of his diverse reading, from his boundless imagination, there arose a crowd of images, nebulous and strange, that he strove to capture in the web of poetry his mind was weaving in every moment of solitude. Solitude was not often available at the Lime Street cottage and because he wanted to be alone he went away for a few days in the second week of October. Ill-health was another reason. Charles Lloyd who paid a visit to Alfoxden in mid-September, at the same time as the Wedgwood brothers, found Coleridge very unwell with a sore throat. During his time at Nether Stowey, and throughout his life he suffered from many ailments that turned him into a hypochondriac. In addition to neuralgia and rheumatism, he suffered frequent bowel attacks, as he called them, which were accompanied by such pains that friends at Stowey testified they had seen him writhing on the ground. Although Coleridge attributed these attacks to various causes like bathing in a cold sea or to eating apple-tart and greens, he himself came to recognise that they started after intense emotional upset, especially after quarrels. His strife with Mrs Coleridge gave him terrible bouts only two or three years later. He had a remedy that he grew to find indispensable, with devastating effect on his whole life and career.

For his neuralgia or toothache he took laudanum. For his dysentery he took opium. He took it for the first time, two grains, 'to check a dysentery', in the fall of the year 1797—his own words —when he had walked to Porlock and up from Porlock Weir through the hanging woods of Culbone, fiery with autumn glory, through the sunless combe and over sheep-speckled fields rising to high Exmoor, spread out in all the splendour of rusting bracken under autumn sunlight. Here he came to Ash Farm that his

Porlock acquaintance must have told him about, a solitary, sturdy farmhouse of rude grey stone standing a quarter of a mile above diminutive Culbone church that served several such solitary farms. Perhaps he saw, as one can today, a stag's great antlers nailed over the opening of the cart-shed and looking like brown branches. From his window beneath the gable, or from the field, if he climbed the stile to walk by night, he saw the woods, the rocks, the sands, the sea beyond Porlock, lying silent under the autumn moon. These are mirrored in a passage from *Osorio* written shortly after his stay.

As usual he carried a book with him. It was *Purchas's Pilgrimage*, a big volume. He sat reading it downstairs at the farmhouse after taking the two grains of opium for his malady. He passed into a trance-like reverie of several hours' duration and dreamed his strange vision of Kubla Khan's palace in Xanadu. He emerged from his reverie, still in a state where the tangible world hardly existed, and poured onto paper fifty of the lines his brain had created under the narcotic's influence while his body rested. Several months later when he took laudanum—opium dissolved in alcohol—for unbearable toothache, he wrote that the repose it conferred was divine, an enchantment, a green spot of fountains and flowers and trees in the very heart of a waste of sands. Opium induced an even stronger enchantment. But when 'a person from Porlock' called at Ash Farm to see him 'on business'; the spell broke. The greater part of the poem could no more be captured than the shapes of dissolving mist. The poem's imagery is that of the opium-dreamer. After this amazing interlude of lotus-eating he returned to his cottage in Lime Street, to his domestic chores, to finishing *Osorio* which Sheridan rejected, to writing his weekly guinea article for the *Morning Post*, which always took two days, and to his ever-mounting worries about money as well as to his wife's anxiety, if not her reproaches, concerning the wherewithal for their bread and cheese.

Quite literally the Coleridges were often shillingless, as Coleridge put it. Sometimes Coleridge had to appeal for the loan of a guinea from Poole or Mr Estlin, or he would ask for an advance £5 from the fund Poole had organised. He never tried to borrow from his friend John Cruickshank as the latter continually mismanaged his own financial affairs. He repaid these loans only to find himself as hard-pressed as ever. The word must have gone round Nether Stowey by Christmas that the Coleridges were in debt to the shopkeepers. In desperation, Coleridge, early in the new year, totted up what he owed. There was a quarter's rent of £2 2s for his cottage, which should have been paid to Mrs Rendle by Christmas Day; there was a quarter's allowance of £5 5s owing to his mother-in-law Mrs Fricker, and there was £5 due to Biggs, the printer of his poems. On top of these large sums he owed Nanny £1 1s of her wages, he owed the Stowey shoemaker £1 13s and the Stowey chandler or general supplier 12s. He owed £2 6s for coal and 12s for the usual pathetic sundries. When he added up and faced the dreadful total £18 11s as he sat at the parlour table with quill and ink-bottle he also faced his decisions. He must accept the offer of the Unitarian ministry at Shrewsbury. This would give him a house and the unknown riches of £120 per annum, although it would deprive him of Tom Poole, his irreplaceable friend. Before going for 'a trial run' at Shrewsbury, he must clear off this debt. He would do this by borrowing £15 from two Bristol friends, and he would sell his ballad to a magazine editor called Richard Phillips who *might* pay him £5 for it.

His ballad—he was writing the 'Ancient Mariner'. On 13 November he and the two Wordsworths had done one of those things that made the inhabitants of Holford stare at them with suspicion about their motives or—after these were allayed—with stern disapproval for such foolish ways. They set off on a sudden impulse through the mists and thickening dusk at half-past four in the afternoon intent on a lonely walk of several days' duration. They followed the brown track on the top of the hills above Alfoxden with the scent of soaked brown bracken and dead black heather impregnating the damp air and with the cries of rooks and gulls rising from the fields below. As long as daylight lasted they could see the misted grey sea away on their right and even the faint pinpricks of lights on the distant Welsh shore. In their twenties, happy and absorbed in one another's company, they laughed and talked as they tramped along, William as usual more reserved than the others, and because they were hard-up they planned for the two men to write jointly a ballad that would earn the expenses of their journey. Ultimately this project became Coleridge's own. They dropped down from the hills at Staple near to St Audries (West Quantoxhead) and by that time darkness must have been gathering so that they chose the road to Watchet rather than a winding path along the shore. At Watchet they stayed the night. The ballad's subject had been discussed en route by the three of them and the working-in of Cruickshank's weird dream decided on. In the little ancient port Coleridge's eye seized on various features that should figure in the ballad's background. Next morning at low tide Wordsworth noticed that the movements of the sea had printed a pattern like ribbing on the dull brown sand. They walked inland after that to return by way of Dulverton.

Now, decided Coleridge in January, the ballad must be finished quickly and sold for what it would fetch in order to clear him of debt. With remarkable strength of conscience he declined a most generous offer from the Wedgwood brothers, because he thought it would entail writing with a political bias, and journeyed to Shrewsbury on borrowed money. As his reputation as a preacher had preceded him he preached to large, enthusiastic congregations in the Unitarian chapel at Shrewsbury. Young, eager William Hazlitt, son of the minister at Wem, walked over to hear him and invited him for a short stay at his father's house where they gave Coleridge a good meal of roast Welsh mutton and the boy hung on every word he uttered. Shrewsbury Unitarians offered Coleridge the post of minister. He was almost committed when, for him, an incredible miracle happened. The two Wedgwoods offered him an annuity of £150 for the rest of his life with no conditions whatever attached. That morning Coleridge trod on air. He was relieved of all worry about providing his family with a house and bread and cheese. He would have freedom to stretch his wings, to write what he pleased and in his own time. His letters to friends and to the Wedgwoods themselves overflowed with the exuberance of his relief and with a determination to produce work that should justify the Wedgwoods' faith in him.

After a short stay with the Wedgwoods at the home of their banker brother, he slept a night at the White Lion Inn in Bristol. Next morning he woke early and walked out to pass the time before an appointment. A dread that something was wrong at

Page 107 Two portraits by John Chubb of the Earl of Egmont: *(above)* when young; *(below)* when older

Page 108 Two portraits by John Chubb: *(left)* Sir Philip Hales of Brymore—Coleridge's 'titled Dogberry';

(right) William Cruickshank of Enmore, agent to the Earl of Egmont, and father of John Cruickshank of Nether Stowey

Nether Stowey haunted him. The Bridgwater coach came rattling over the cobbles. 'Will you get in, sir?' the coachman asked. He got in and went home where he found that all was well. However his financial cares rushed back to frighten him for, in the way of people who never had to worry about money, the Wedgwoods had not understood his need for the immediate advance of a few pounds. Coleridge was down to his last penny. The Wedgwood annuity did away with the fund to which kindly friends had subscribed and a refund must be made to Mr Estlin. He could borrow no more from Poole as he owed him £5 5s borrowed to help some impecunious friend. Biggs the printer, and Sara's mother absolutely must receive their dues so that £10 had to be raised immediately. 'As to myself, I can contrive to go on here.' He decided to offer himself as minister to the Dampiet Street chapel in Bridgwater, although he expected little remuneration. Just in time, the arrival of some Wedgwood money solved his problems.

In spite of a tormenting quarrel with his brother-in-law Southey, and Charles Lloyd who was its main cause, the next few months were Coleridge's truly golden time. Both for him and the Wordsworths it was a season of nearly unflawed happiness as Wordsworth's *Prelude* shows equally with the journal Dorothy Wordsworth kept during those enchanted days (known as the *Alfoxden Journal*). Only the entries from January to May 1798 exist. During that period the three were constantly together, or Coleridge and Dorothy were on their own, indoors or out, in any sort of weather, at any time of day until well after midnight. He called her 'exquisite in mind and heart', 'Wordsworth's exquisite sister', without thinking of her looks. The perfect communication between their two spirits reveals itself in the journal entries for the period during which Coleridge was writing 'Christabel'.

Both Coleridge and Wordsworth were working throughout these first months of 1798 writing the poems destined with the 'Ballad of the Ancient Mariner' to be united in a volume entitled *Lyrical Ballads*. In March Coleridge brought his finished 'Ancient Mariner' to Alfoxden and read it aloud in his sonorous voice by the parlour fire. He wrote several of the poems he called Conversation poems, a genre in which he excelled. He wrote 'The Nightingale' and his beautiful 'Fears in Solitude' reflecting the

G

fear inspired in remote Somerset villages by the threat of French invasion. Back in February he had written his 'Frost at Midnight' as he sat in the parlour of his cottage while the fire sank low and his baby slept near him in the cradle and he looked through the small window-panes at Lime Street roofs gleaming with frost under the moon. He still preached from time to time for Mr Howel and Dr Toulmin.

Spring came tardily that year; both the journal and 'Christabel' say so. Then it broke over the Somerset landscape in sudden glory. In May Coleridge tempted Cottle down on a visit from Bristol, promising an excursion to Lynton and Lynmouth in all their May pride. Cottle accepted and did the walk with Coleridge and Wordsworth in the last week of May. They visited the Valley of Stones, as the Wordsworths and Coleridge always called the Valley of Rocks, that strange half-savage place of vast rocks, sands and caves haunted by screaming sea-birds, that seized Coleridge's imagination. After Cottle's return to Bristol Coleridge walked alone to Lynton in one day and back to Stowey the next.

Immediately after Cottle's visit young William Hazlitt came, at Coleridge's invitation, for a visit lasting three weeks. In justice to Sara Coleridge it should be remembered that her baby Berkeley was only between two and three weeks old when Coleridge brought these visitors for her to look after. Hazlitt spent several days of his holiday over at Alfoxden. Coleridge set off with him to walk yet again to Lynton in sunny June weather, and this time Coleridge's dogged admirer John Chester went with them. He was a young man of Tom Poole's age who lived with his widowed mother and several brothers and sisters in a house not far from Coleridge's. He was short, thick-set and bow-legged with a slightly dragging walk like a cattle-drover's, and wore a countryman's brown corduroys, brown coat and boots. He carried a hazel-switch from a hedge and kept up determinedly with Coleridge's quick walk, intent on every word that fell from his lips. As usual talk flowed from Coleridge like a tireless stream. After leaving the Quantocks they made a wide detour and showed Hazlitt Dunster lying down below on their right, and looking to Hazlitt's charmed eyes 'as clear, as pure, as embrowned' in the summer sunlight as any landscape by Gaspard Poussin. ('Embrowned' is an adjective

Dorothy used also.) Later in the day, as they tramped to Lynton to the tune of Coleridge's voice, Hazlitt saw near Blue Anchor and Minehead—or perhaps only thought he saw, with the imagination of a twenty-year-old boy excited by local stories he had heard in a Stowey inn or over the cider-mugs at Poole's—several of the smugglers who at that time brought their kegs of brandy into little creeks like Kilve Pill or hid them in the Watchet caves. Later, from a vantage point on a high brown heath, Hazlitt pointed out to Coleridge the black silhouette of a ship on the far horizon where the red orb of the setting sun could be seen framed by the masts in a way that recalled the skeleton ship and the peering, burning sun of the 'Ancient Mariner'. The three men slept two nights at Lynton and Coleridge took Hazlitt to see the Valley of Rocks that he thought of using for the background of his 'Wanderings of Cain'.

On the Sunday when Hazlitt was due to leave Stowey, Coleridge walked over the hills to preach at Mary Street chapel in Taunton. Afterwards he went on to Bridgwater where he had a rendezvous with Hazlitt and where Mr Howel probably put them up for the night. Next day they walked to Bristol together, talking most of the way, and Hazlitt went home to Shropshire. Coleridge spent a day with Mr Estlin who vainly tried to dissuade him from his plan of leaving his wife and family three or four months in Stowey on their own while he went on a tour in Germany with John Chester and the Wordsworths, whose notice to leave Alfoxden had nearly expired. From Bristol, Coleridge visited the Wedgwoods at their home in Surrey from where he wrote to Tom Poole: 'This place is a noble large house in a rich pleasant country, but the little Toe of Quantock is better than the head and shoulders of Surry and Middlesex'.

The Wordsworths final departure was a huge grief to Coleridge, mitigated only by thoughts of the German trip. He did not see how he could live away from them and was permanently embittered towards those Somerset Tory squires who had campaigned against them. For a time Coleridge had hoped to find the Wordsworths a furnished house near Stowey. Whatever he felt about Dorothy, he could not endure to lose the companionship of a man and poet he regarded as the embodiment of greatness, and in anguish he declared to Poole that if they let Wordsworth go, the very hills, woods, streams, the sea and shores, near Stowey and Holford, would break forth into reproaches.

William and Dorothy spent a last week at the Lime Street cottage before departing to Bristol. How did Sara Coleridge feel as the others discussed their joyful plans round her parlour table? Perhaps she did not mind overmuch as she was engrossed by her young children, was supposedly provided for and had the ever-faithful Poole to lean upon. Coleridge had explained that he was leaving her for only three or four months in order to learn German properly. If events prospered he might even fetch his family.

The links with Nether Stowey remained strong while Coleridge, after leaving the Wordsworths, toured Germany in a frugal fashion with John Chester. He said that the trip 'from Stowey to Stowey ultimately cost £90', very much more than he had calculated, but this was not surprising as his intended four months' absence stretched from September 1798 to July 1799. He hung on the post for Poole's letters and wrote in return long letters full of great affection. When letters were held up, his own to Poole carried reproaches and fears that he had been forgotten; Poole must go to the Lime Street cottage with messages for Sara and kiss the two infants for Coleridge. For his part Poole looked eagerly for letters from Germany and shared them with Thomas Ward who early began to transcribe them. On the arrival of a Hamburg letter in Castle Street young Ward leapt up in excitement and twirled like a whirligig, knocking Poole's table and chairs so that two brimming glasses of beer splashed their contents while the bread and the cheese slid about on the board. Coleridge wrote that he was saving up many anecdotes to relate when he next sat in Poole's great armchair and drank his strong beer.

As for Sara, Coleridge sent her long, vivacious descriptive letters in which he called her his dear, dear love, declared that he thought of her every night, that he panted to be back at Stowey, to clasp her and his children to his heart, and that he wished she was with him. Coping with life at the cottage throughout autumn and winter, Sara must have swallowed these protestations with a grain of salt, especially when they were coupled with accounts of

skating, of invitations to dinner and concerts and with such statements as 'I am pressed by all the ladies to dance' even though the
statement was hastily qualified by another that he was in no
dancing mood. It soon became plain that Coleridge felt in no hurry
to get back to Stowey and that he did not worry when her main-
tenance money had nearly run out. He airily assured her that if it
was not convenient for Poole to advance her a little, Poole would
write to Wedgwood on her behalf. Indeed she would have fared
badly at times but for Poole's unflagging kindness.

Yet Coleridge remembered certain things. The colours of the
clouds in the night sky at Hamburg were 'quite English' and
reminded him of bringing Sara home from Poole's with his arm
round her as they looked up at a summer sky. He remembered the
white cloak she wore in the street as he passed German women
clad in striped ones. And while the mists and rains of winter
came on he shuddered to remember the disadvantages of the
cottage he had been so set on acquiring two years before. Lime
Street would be so deep in mud that it would have turned into a
real Slough of Despond, 'an impassable hog-stye' in fact. He
wrote this to Sara, pitying her for living there and for having the
voices of the Poorhouse Nightingales in her ears—an allusion to
the penniless occupants of the little cottage poorhouse in Lime
Street. Quite suddenly he realised that he hated the thought of
ever living again in the cramped and primitive dwelling he had
occupied for eighteen months. He wrote to Poole that it was
impossible for him to be either comfortable or useful in a house
as small as the Lime Street cottage. He did not consider it too early
for Poole to be looking round for another and if Woodlands
could be obtained at a reasonable rent he would like to take it.
He meant the spacious white house set in parkland off the road
leading to Holford. Wordsworth, Coleridge added, was torn
between living near Stowey and in the north of England, but
objected to the lack of library facilities in Stowey as he thought
little of the Bristol library and in the north could use a gentleman's private one. Coleridge on the other hand wanted only old
books which Bristol could supply, and anyway he could not con-
template leaving Poole or Stowey.

Poole tolerantly replied that for a long time he had thought the

Lime Street house unsuitable, refraining from reminding Coleridge that he had thought so from the first. Perhaps Coleridge would consider the house that Philip Hancock used to live in? It had a fine, secluded room adjoining its garden; had access to fields, was rented for £16. But Coleridge raised every possible objection to living in Hancock's house: he did not want to live right *in* Stowey (the old cottage was at the far end) nor right *in* any town; towns were bad, physically and morally, for children. Besides, Stowey people disliked him and all his household. And in the house opposite Hancock's lived widowed Mrs Richard Poole who was so rude to Mrs Coleridge. All the same, if no house could be found just outside Stowey he would accept Hancock's.

At this time Sara was living in Bristol at her mother's, where the baby Berkeley died, perhaps from the effects of his inoculation by the Stowey surgeon. She wrote a heartrending letter to Poole and implored him to break the news to Coleridge, which Poole did. Sara had to ask Poole to send her some money to buy 'a few things' in Bristol that she needed for her return to Stowey; she was returning without kind Nanny, so much regretted. Coleridge's grateful reply to Poole contained a cutting reference to Stowey people in general and to Poole's servants in particular: they were all sunk in depravity. He wrote tenderly to Sara; far away from home he could see the baby's cradle standing in a corner of their Lime Street bedroom, see the baby Berkeley in it. Yet he answered Sara testily when she asked about his return. She must understand that he was *working*, preparing a translation of Lessing. He would return in June and couldn't reach Stowey quickly enough to please him. He only wished it were possible for his ship to put in at Shurton Bars where he had written his lines about Sara shortly before their marriage. He enclosed a set of verses 'If I had but two little wings' that told her he fled to her in his sleep.

By May, Coleridge felt suddenly homesick. The leafless woods made him long for the Somerset spring and to hear Poole's whistle to the blackbirds. The German nightingales, actually singing in snow, made him recall the idyllic spring of the previous year when he listened, in Dorothy Wordsworth's company, to the singing of the nightingale in the Alfoxden grove and wrote his poem 'The Nightingale'. By this time Wordsworth had firmly decided to live in the north of England and Coleridge himself had made up his mind that he still wanted a home near Stowey, even Hancock's house if he had no choice. 'My dear Poole, I am homesick.' 'My Resolve is fixed, *not to leave you till you leave me.*' Characteristically, to suit his case, Coleridge reversed his previous arguments. It would be wrong to move Sara to a place where she had no friends; there was the question of removal expenses, an unwarrantable outlay. He still hoped that Wordsworth might return to Somerset, sooner or later, to Alfoxden even. This hope was finally quenched in September 1799 when Wordsworth relinquished for ever the intention of trying to live there a second time.

Coleridge and Chester arrived home in Nether Stowey towards the end of July. Coleridge was extremely worried because his chests of clothes and valuable books had not arrived from Germany. Southey and his wife Edith, Mrs Coleridge's sister, came over from Minehead where they had been lodging at a Mr Holloway's, and made a few days' stay at the cottage in Lime Street as a token that the old quarrel, smoothed down by Tom Poole, had been finally forgotten. After this visit the Coleridges and the Southeys departed to the much more comfortable Southey home at Exeter whence the two husbands did a short walking-tour in Devon. The views from Totnes and Dartmoor impressed Coleridge but while admitting this he declared that the rest of Devon seemed to him very tame when compared to 'Quantock, Porlock, Culbone, Linton', seeming to forget that Lynton lay outside Somerset. He wrote to Tom Poole that the loan of five guineas would greatly oblige him and that he was very anxious to settle the matter of a new house.

Domestic trials submerged him, not to mention Sara, as soon as they found themselves back again under the cottage roof on 24 September. They had just acquired, to Sara's relief, a new maid named Fanny, who was not destined to replace much-mourned Nanny in their affections. She brought with her that impolitely named disease of the dirty, the itch, and three-year-old Hartley seemed to have caught the infection. Fanny was sent packing. Mrs Coleridge, beside herself, moaned and complained incessantly while carrying out the apothecary's advice to anoint

Hartley liberally with a sulphur preparation. (The child, with his merry disposition, sang, laughed and slept. Coleridge temporarily nick-named him Brimstonello.) The parents acquired for their own use the preventive contraptions called mercurial girdles which made them stink to high heaven. This exasperated Coleridge into going for a long walk in the rain to lessen the stench. He got very wet while sweating profusely. This aggravated the stink he carried around and made him cast off his girdle in fury. He immediately developed redhot rheumatism in his back, arms and neck so that he decided to go to the Wedgwoods at Upcott to recuperate. Sickness and sleeplessness drove him back home where he felt at peace only when sunk in his chair near the fire while he read by the light of his usual solitary candle one of the old folios that could enthrall him for many nights. Sara and Hartley slept. 'The silence of the silent house is most delightful' he wrote. Yet he could still be the gayest of companions and create laughter all around him.

Gaiety had deserted him for the time being even though it still sparkled in his letters. The house reeked of sulphur. Mrs Coleridge started the great upheaval of washing all the sheets and blankets, washing clothes and burying them in the garden, washing the house throughout. She had no one to help her unless old Mrs Rich came in and it was just at this time that the Riches lived in terror of their insane son. What with heavy rain and constant washing Coleridge declared that their hovel could float away at any minute. He did notice that Sara had tired herself to death. Even Hartley, luckily in good health, had turned cross, noisy and mischievous with being shut up indoors. Coleridge made the excuse that he must make inquiries in Bristol about his lost luggage from Germany and thankfully escaped. His boxes arrived safely in Stowey only two days later and Sara, with Hartley, went for a well-earned rest at the home of Poole's friends the Newtons, Old Cleeve vicarage, not far from Watchet. The Rev James Newton, born at Withycombe, had been curate at Stowey in his youth. He was a considerable scholar and once got involved in argument with Dr Johnson on a coach journey. When Sara returned in November to reopen the cottage that still reeked of sulphur, she expected to find her husband staying at Poole's. But he had gone north from Bristol, travelling with Joseph Cottle to the Hutchinsons' farm at Sockburn where the Wordsworths were staying.

He never went back to live in the Lime Street cottage. Deep down within himself, although he had not reached the point of openly admitting it, he knew that never again after tasting the freedom of his life abroad with nagging domestic cares forgotten, could he settle down to a humdrum restricted life with Sara, whose temperament was so hopelessly incompatible with his own, in that pokey inconvenient cottage where he could never get away from the sound of her voice or from Hartley's noise. Moreover he realised that he had an overwhelming need of the stimulus that Wordsworth's company provided. Already they were discussing the poetry each was engaged on and looking forward to producing greater work, in spite of the failure of the *Lyrical Ballads*, 'not liked by any' as Mrs Coleridge had candidly, if waspishly, remarked, in 1798 when the little volume reached an unappreciative public. Coleridge might continue to think of Poole as his anchor, his well-beloved friend, but Poole had no profound understanding of a poet's mind and could not provide the essential stimulus for a poet's work. Coleridge walked with his friends in the Lake District and professed to see some resemblance to the Quantock Hills in the tracts of heathery moorland. He came to Grasmere and fell in love with its beauty. He started falling in love with another girl called Sara, the attractive and intelligent sister of Wordsworth's future wife, Mary Hutchinson. But he did not shelve his responsibilities. He accepted a five-month engagement to write for the *Morning Post*, took London lodgings and sent money to Stowey for Sara and Hartley to join him, forgetting his former professed belief that life in towns was a bad thing, especially for children. Tom Poole wrote to him; he felt wounded that he had not been consulted, he was a little jealous of Wordsworth, but his friendship stayed loyal and deeply affectionate. Coleridge assuerd him that he would ultimately return to Stowey where he had left his books and furniture, but that he must insist on a house large enough to provide him with a study well away from the noise of women and children. It must have a garden. Would Poole continue to look out for one?

Not very long after leaving Stowey, Sara took Hartley on a six-week visit to Mrs Roskilly who had moved to Gloucestershire. Finding a house needed to be hurried up as Sara expected another child in the summer of 1800. Once more Coleridge thought of the lovely spacious house at Alfoxden and suggested that the Southeys could share it with them. Nothing came of this. He continued wishing that Wordsworth would retake it, but Wordsworth had decisively taken Dove Cottage. Poole suggested that the Coleridges should rent half a farmhouse. They would have to share the kitchen with the other tenants. Coleridge recoiled in horror at the prospect of hearing Sara and a young servant squabbling with the farmer's wife over kitchen facilities. It would be fifty times worse than the old hovel in Lime Street he told the long-suffering Poole. He began to think of taking lodgings in Minehead or Porlock for the summer if Poole could not get them a house. He himself remained adamant on one point: he was not coming back to Lime Street. The last project to be put forward was the taking of a house at Aisholt, that beautiful little village with red fields, lanes full of primroses and runnels of water, farmhouses built of red sandstone, thatched cottages and red sandstone church; in its sheltered Quantock combe, it is fairly isolated even today when factory farming has encroached there. Coleridge himself felt tempted by the thatched cottage in 'a deep romantic chasm' that slanted down a green hill. This cottage may have been the old School House, occupied in the 1920s by Sir Henry Newbolt. However this time Mrs Coleridge rebelled with some violence. She could not live in a place so remote and lonely, she must have a town and a little life. 'The situation is delicious' wrote Coleridge, 'but Sara being Sara and I being I, we must live in a town or close to one so that she may have neighbours and acquaintances. God knows where we can go, for the situation which suits me does not suit my wife.'

He came to Poole's for a few days that June and went house-hunting at Porlock to no avail. With Sara's confinement near he knew that he must do what in his heart he really preferred; he must move north to the Lake District.

He parted from Poole with dejection. He said that he would have given Nether Stowey his preference if a suitable house could have been found, but there was only his old cottage which simply would not do. He owed it to himself and his work to be sure of one quiet room. After leaving he admitted that he had sometimes suffered considerably at the cottage in Lime Street; he had known 'the utter desolation which a small and inconvenient house spread through my literary efforts and hourly comforts' and he had experienced 'the contagious fretfulness of the weaker vessels in my family'.

So in June 1800, the Coleridges and their little son finally went north to live. Neither Coleridge nor Sara was ever so happy again as they had been under that despised Somerset roof.

CHAPTER 5

LATER VISITS TO NETHER STOWEY

For several months preceding his twenty-ninth birthday in October 1801 Coleridge suffered from various severe illnesses, of which the chief were his old enemies rheumatism and what he called 'bilious colic'. He had long spells in bed and treated his ills with opium and brandy that gave sweet relief while bringing black depression in their train. Money ran very short. Discord with poor Sara increased as his attachment to Sara Hutchinson strengthened. During this time the ever-generous Tom Poole sent him several invitations to stay with him at Nether Stowey. Finally he sent Coleridge £25 to pay for the journey from Keswick, to settle bills, and to provide Mrs Coleridge with £5. Coleridge travelled to London in November where friends found him lodgings with another Mr Howell whose wife nursed him through another fearful bout of colic. At Christmas, when Coleridge dined with Humphry Davy, Mr Howell lent him £5 and, for his journey on the top of the Bridgwater Mail Coach, an enormous thick water-proof cloak called a roquelaire that had cost seven guineas when the government issued it to a member of the expedition to Quiberon. Coleridge had cause to bless this garment and Mr Howell during the eighteen-hour journey to Bath through torren-tial rain, thunder and lightning. He stayed with Tom Poole for a month in the company of Tom Wedgwood. The congenial com-panionship of Wedgwood, Poole and Ward coupled with careful diet and temporary lack of harassment calmed him and gradually cured his 'bowel-attacks'. In spite of a prolonged spell of hard frost which he detested he returned to London in better health. On the last Sunday night in Stowey he wrote a hurried and prosaic letter to his wife Sara to say that he hoped to God she had made herself flannel drawers and was taking mustard pills as a defence against the winter cold. That same night he wrote one of his earliest letters to Sara Hutchinson—perhaps the first. This love-affair lasted ten years and was not physically consummated. Coleridge's stern views on sexual morality were expressed to Poole at this time when he warmly commended a Stowey youth for doing the right thing by a pregnant girl, that is, marrying her, in spite of malignant opposition from Richard Symes the attorney. Coleridge declared that the youth's manly conduct had saved the Stowey girl from becoming a whore and that most Stowey youths were 'deep-dyed whoremongers'. The hubbub would die down . . . 'husband and wife are husband and wife'.

During this winter visit Coleridge confided to Tom Wedgwood something of the troubles that beset him. Chief among these was the failure of his marriage. Mrs Coleridge by this time upset him with scenes of screaming temper, or so he alleged. It is surprising that Coleridge found unnatural her jealousy of Sara Hutchinson and her resentment of his strong intimacy with the Wordsworths from which she was excluded. Love for his children still restrained him from definite separation. Discord increased during 1802 when Mrs Coleridge was pregnant again, but the incompatible pair still tried to mend their marriage while Coleridge protested that she must not be jealous of his loving or of his being beloved else-where. Ailing, hypochondriac, taking opium, full of diet theories, longing for a warm climate, Coleridge left her for several weeks just before the birth of his daughter, to accompany Tom Wedgwood, who himself took opium to relieve spells of intense suffering, on a most enjoyable visit to the lively Allen family who were connected by marriage with the Wedgwoods. From their supremely comfortable house at Crescelly in south Wales, Coleridge wrote to Poole, just back from Paris and not as well as usual. Coleridge's old gaiety sparkled from the letter. He teased Poole about the question of clotted cream, the 'clouted cream' that Devon-born Coleridge could eat in great quantities. He had enjoyed it at Crescelly without stint and without any bad-tempered glances; at other houses where likewise they kept a dairy, he had always received, he told Poole, looks that could have curdled all the cream in the dish if he ate only three pennyworth of it, even though six shillingsworth of wine was never grudged. Poole accepted this criticism of his watchful dairymaid, and of himself, in good part.

An unexpected little scene marred one evening at the Allens'. It was caused by Coleridge's rather tiresome fondness for reading Wordsworth's poems aloud. Dorothy Wordsworth had recently made a copy of William's poem 'The Leech Gatherer' specially for him and he carried it to Crescelly. Unluckily the gay girl Fanny Allen went into shrieks of mirth on hearing him read a bathetic stanza that was afterwards omitted; this set the other girls laughing immoderately, including Kitty Wedgwood who always found Coleridge conceited. Folding up the manuscript, Coleridge cuttingly remarked 'Of course the poem seems absurd to a person of no genius'. Tom Wedgwood had to make the peace.

By this time Tom Poole had moved into his second house at Nether Stowey and let the Castle Street house to Thomas Ward. At the close of the year 1802 Tom Wedgwood wrote to him that he and Coleridge intended to pay him a visit in order to see how comfortable they could make themselves in his new house. In the first week of February 1803 Coleridge arrived at Stowey alone, because Wedgwood felt too ill to travel. Coleridge himself was ailing and literally under the weather, 'miserably afflicted by the cold' he wrote to Poole before his arrival. His letter carried advance requests for a roomy bedroom, with a fire in it and if possible a chaise to meet him in Bridgwater when he left the Bristol coach. His host met all these demands. Coleridge was laid low by colic for a day or two and then revived to enjoy the solid comfort of Poole's house, the lovely wood fire in his bedroom, the cheerful attention of a bright nine-year-old boy who waited on him and was pleased with a penny. He wrote to Wedgwood that warm rooms, the company of an old friend and above all, tranquillity, cured his complaint. But his mind was far from tranquil. He was torn by the wish not to return to Keswick and his wife, and had half-resolved to travel to a warmer climate as Tom Wedgwood's companion. Moreover he had grasped the grim fact that he could no longer do without opium although dependence on it was under-mining his health, his capacity to work, his whole life. Not for nothing did he call himself a crumbling wall undermined at its foundation. Both he and his friends were aware of the terrible change six years had brought about in the young poet who had come to live in Nether Stowey in the New Year of 1797. Yet *a poet* Coleridge substantially remained. At this time he asserted that he did not think any pains whatever could eat out of his being the love and joy towards 'hills and rocks and steep waters'. How-ever he felt happy and content in this bachelor household with an old woman and the child to wait on him as he sat writing letters by the crackling fire in his bedroom while Poole busied himself downstairs or out-of-doors with his manifold occupations. Poole told Coleridge that he would send Wedgwood's brother fifty bushels of the finest malt, bright-coloured if it was for ale, pale-coloured if for making beer. But for Southey he would obtain and despatch a local delicacy that Southey had undoubtedly enjoyed in Porlock—the pickled seaweed known as laver.

Listening at night to Poole's rich Somerset voice talking about these homely matters, planning with Poole their coming joint visit to the Wedgwood house at Tarrant Gunville, Coleridge was more and more impressed by Poole's essential goodness and incorrupt-ibility. However he felt vexed with him for refusing to hire a chaise when they set out for Dorset via Taunton on a Friday morning. Poole obstinately insisted on hiring a 'one-horse chair' that broke down several times so that they arrived on Sunday afternoon in the rain instead of on the Friday evening.

Coleridge carried with him a four-ounce packet that Poole had frowned on when it arrived in Stowey by post. It was a packet of the drug called Bang (Bhang) prepared from powdered leaves of Indian hemp, the nepenthe of classical mythology. He had pro-cured this while in Stowey for poor Tom Wedgwood to try in the hope of alleviating his pain. Coleridge too meant to try it. He would not trust this precious packet to Milton or the other Stowey carrier for transport into Bridgwater and posting. By this time he had made up his mind that the Stowey carriers were worse than careless, they were thieving rogues who deserved to end up on the gallows. In fact he felt antagonistic enough towards Stowey people to declare that every one of them except Poole and Ward ought to go to hell. He still had small wrangles with Poole over the quantity of quill-pens he expected to find ready for his use and about Poole's unwillingness to put ink in the bedroom. Yet Poole's warm welcome and liberal hospitality never failed. In April 1803 he wrote to Coleridge that if he thought the south of England better for his health he must come back to Stowey. Indeed, he pressed Coleridge to come by holding out the bait of his new 'nice, very nice' bookroom.

It was over four years before Coleridge came again and then it was for the last time.

Six months before, he had returned from a two-years' stay on Malta. His friend Tom Wedgwood, so brilliantly talented, had died in his absence, leaving a will that contained the bequest of 'An annuity for life of £75 to Samuel Taylor Coleridge, now or late of Nether Stowey, Gentleman', yet Coleridge still remained curiously inert about writing to Tom's brother, his other bene-factor. On this score even Poole reproved him when he came to Stowey. He was more deeply in love with Sara Hutchinson than ever and had resolved not to live with his wife any longer, but as he was determined to show her proper respect he brought her and his three children (Hartley aged 10, Derwent, 6, Sara 4½) on a visit to his clergyman-schoolmaster brother in Devon. The latter had promised to pay the expenses of the journey. However, Coleridge wrote from Bristol to tell him of the proposed separation which so scandalised the Rev George Coleridge that he refused to pay any expenses or to receive his brother and family as visitors. This put Coleridge to great difficulties. He brought his family to Poole's in June. The visit was to last a fortnight but lengthened to over two months with a few breaks when Coleridge alone, or all of them, spent several days with other friends. For the children Poole's easy bachelor establishment and the lovely Quantock country in full summer made a paradise they never forgot. 'The children talk evermore of the happiness at Stowey' said Mrs Coleridge afterwards. Coleridge himself derived great physical benefit from this holiday, especially during the later period spent alone with Poole. He and Poole rode miles through the steep tortuous lanes where bracken and foxgloves stood high. He

Page 125 Alfoxden House or Alfoxton Park

Page 126 The dog-pound near Alfoxden gates. The cottage of Christopher Trickey (Simon Lee) stood nearby

wandered the Quantocks and around Alfoxden on what he sentimentally called dear old walks. He abstained from drinking spirits
and contented himself with Poole's strong beer and cider: Poole
made cider from the apples in his new orchards, but sometimes
they drank the golden pippin cider made by his uncle in Taunton.

Wanderings round Quantock villages in Poole's company
occasioned the scribbling by Coleridge of some humorous verse
on the back of a letter he handed to Poole who endorsed it. ' "On
my Walks" Written by Col, September 1807'. Coleridge thought
Poole's fond attachment to his relatives one of his few defects;
Coleridge could not be expected to like the Rev John Poole and
his disapproving sisters who from 1803 all lived in the new
Enmore Vicarage, now the attractive Poole House. Coleridge
declared that whether they walked to Puriton (called Perriton
then) to Cummage (Combwich) or to Stogursey, their walks
always had to bring them circuitously to Enmore. In fact he
declared, facetiously, a new wall map marking these novel routes
would soon be published. He himself grew fond of this pleasant
village with its ferny red-banked lanes full of red hawthorns and
its red sandstone cottages.

These weeks in Poole's company, days of roaming a lovely
countryside under blue summer skies, the green solitude of the
familiar hills and combes where he encountered only the whortle-
berry-pickers, the lonely charcoal-burners, the woodmen with
laden ponies, benefited his health so much that he wrote to
Humphry Davy in London to say that he felt prepared to under-
take giving a course of lectures at the Royal Institution, an honour
that Davy had procured him with suitable fees attached. He told
Davy that even his load of overwhelming despair and self-disgust
had started to lift. He did not admit to Davy that these were
caused mainly by his opium addiction.

In spite of his improved health he suffered much mental
torment during this last visit. Poole, Ward, the Cruickshanks of
Enmore, the Brices, his correspondents Cottle, Humphry Davy and
Josiah Wedgwood to whom at last he wrote a letter of personal
grief about Tom Wedgwood's death, heard only about his frightful
financial embarrassments, his problems with regard to wife and
children, his recurrent illnesses. He did not confide to any of

these that during this summer visit he was tormented by his uncon-summated love for Sara Hutchinson, but his personal notebook recorded that on 13 September at half-past two in the morning he awoke in his bed at Tom Poole's after suffering in his sleep the pangs of jealousy. He wrote down that he felt jealous even of Wordsworth because not only was he beloved by his wife Mary but greatly loved by his sister-in-law Sara Hutchinson who lived with them. During that anguished night Coleridge wrote that it was not in Wordsworth's nature 'to love *any* being as I love you', with Sara Hutchinson's image in his mind.

He lay one day on the Quantock heather under the boughs of a tree within sight of the sea, listening to the larks and the invisible streamlets as he had done nine years earlier. That day he wrote in his notebook *Recollections of Love*, one of the few truly beautiful poems he wrote after quitting the Lime Street cottage, and in this poem, seemingly forgetful of the unique companionship he had enjoyed with Dorothy Wordsworth during the most blissful months of his life, he expressed his belief that the beloved spirit of Sara Hutchinson whom he had not then met, must have hovered near him when he lay in the heather and heard the Quantock rills and skylarks nine years before. (The poem says eight years.)

On the Friday afternoon before Midsummer Day he almost certainly stood outside Poole's gate in the street now called St Mary Street, and showed his young children the procession of the Nether Stowey Female Friendly Society. The procession today is almost exactly similar but Coleridge was watching the first anniversary ceremony. The women members, wearing summer dresses and carrying bunches of flowers from their gardens, lined up outside the Rose and Crown Inn behind six little girls in white who carried baskets of flowers. They walked in double file along the street beside the brook, headed by a girl who carried a blue banner embroidered with the rhymed motto

> Foresight and Union
> linked
> by Christian Love
> Helped by the Good below
> and Heaven above.

The assertion that Coleridge composed the motto is no more than wishful thinking, like the tradition that Dorothy Wordsworth made the blue banner which still exists but is not used and which Americans once tried to buy. A brass band heralds their approach today and a few players may have mustered in 1807. They all filed up the avenue to the north door of Stowey church where the Rev Mr Northey or his curate preached a special sermon. Afterwards they paraded the village before sitting down to a fine Somerset tea at the Rose and Crown which gentlemen attended. Coleridge, as a close friend of the club's founder, undoubtedly came to this function and enjoyed the clouted cream provided.

John Cruickshank had gone, but Coleridge still enjoyed an affectionate friendship with his younger, unmarried sister Mary. At times he walked to Enmore to visit her, her mother and her brother William, the earl's agent since his father died. He was invited to stay at Enmore Castle, a Gothic pile of red sandstone erected by Lord Egmont's father and given imposing imitation medieval features such as moat, drawbridge and gatehouse. (The castle is now mainly Victorian.) During this visit Coleridge roamed Enmore Park in autumn weather making notes on its venerable trees like the elm five and a quarter yards round, the oak that was 'monstrous . . . gouty . . . double-jointed'.

Certain readers have suggested that the gentle maid 'who dwelleth in her hospitable house Hard by the castle' in Coleridge's poem 'The Nightingale' was meant to denote Mary Cruickshank and that when he named the two girls in his ballad 'The Three Graves' he had in mind Mary and her sister Ellen—married by 1807—whom he was very fond of when she visited her brother and Alfoxden in 1798.

During the course of this visit of Coleridge's, Mary Cruickshank went visiting her friends the Brices at Aisholt Rectory where, with the desire to spread Coleridge's fame as a poet, she borrowed Miss Brice's copy of the first edition of Coleridge's poems to lend Lady Elizabeth Perceval at Enmore Castle. This caused Coleridge great vexation as it contained an early sonnet that might make Lady Elizabeth think he had once held revolutionary principles. He hurriedly wrote to Mary asking her to set this right by lending

Lady Elizabeth Poole's copy of the second edition, which he enclosed.

He wrote her in August a very affectionate note about a visit he himself had paid his friend the Rev John Brice at Aisholt. He had been wandering about on a summer evening in a maze of unfamiliar lanes while his thoughts wandered in a maze of dreams. It occurred to him that he ought to find his way to Stowey and supper and therefore he felt cheered by the sight of a signpost marked 'Stowey' close to a little stone bridge over a stream and by a glimpse of another up in a tree. So he pressed on although the route was unfamiliar, and instead of Stowey reached Aisholt after passing through the hamlet of Plainsfield. The details in the letter are vague but it seems likely that he found the bridge over the stream and the Stowey sign in Spaxton. This bridge spanned the stream just below a mill, then in use but fallen derelict now (*not* the mill by the church, called Splatt Mill). He followed the road as far as Spaxton Lodge, the place where he found four roads meeting, and when he turned left—as he said he did—the road took him past Tuxwell Farm to the hamlet of Plainsfield. Here he recognised a steeply-climbing, high-hedged, narrow lane as a road to Aisholt. This he followed in the direction, for a time, of ancient Durborough Farm until he turned off towards Aisholt Church on the crest of the hill above the 'green romantic chasm' where he had once thought of taking a cottage. At what is now called the Old Rectory the Rev John Brice gave him dinner, where, in spite of the adjurations of the Brice daughters, the two men lingered to consume two bottles of port as well as several glasses of mead while talking, among other matters, of their absent friend John Cruickshank. Coleridge boasted that even in the dark he managed to find his way to Stowey.

Just after his stay in Stowey, he wrote a letter about a book to Mary Cruickshank, although why to her and not Poole is not clear. Coleridge, after his usual custom, had freely annotated the volume with his own comments, thinking that the book belonged to Tom Poole who always encouraged him to write notes in any books from Poole's shelves. This particular copy happened to belong to the Stowey Book Society and Coleridge apologised in dismay. He had probably picked up the volume when visiting the

Cruickshanks. On another occasion he scribbled comments in a religious work Lord Egmont had lent Poole.

An outstanding event of that summer holiday was the unexpected visit of twenty-two year old Thomas De Quincey who, for several years, had been eager to meet this man of brilliant intellect in order to discuss metaphysical and psychological problems which had been De Quincey's favourite studies at Oxford. In the summer of 1807 he was staying at Hotwells near Bristol, and hearing that Coleridge was in Nether Stowey impulsively set off walking southward to find him. By evening he had reached the ferry by which he crossed the river, and walked the six miles to Tom Poole's. De Quincey described this journey so many years afterwards that time had somewhat confused the details in his mind. He wrote that he reached 'a ferry on the river Bridgewater at a village called, I think, Stogursey'. What he really did was to cross the river Parret by the ferry at the village of Pawlett which carried him over to Combwich where, on a signpost, he read the name of Stogursey. He followed the way to Stogursey, past the front of Hill Farm in Otterhampton parish, before striking the road to Nether Stowey. He would *not* go into Stogursey village, but followed the winding lane through Bonson and Fiddington to emerge at the point just off the Minehead road where the pretty but disused old smithy stands. He reached 'the little town of Nether Stowey in the Quantock Hills' and the ever-open door of Poole's house which he thought at first sight old-fashioned, just as he thought that its owner looked an old-fashioned, plain-looking farmer growing stout in his forties. He soon discovered, as many others had, that the exterior of both house and owner was deceptive. The hospitable house possessed comfort, even luxury, with good furniture and an admirable library. The man had travelled, had acquired considerable culture and learning, possessed a liberal outlook, and was dedicated to the welfare of the humblest inhabitants in his neighbourhood.

As Coleridge had gone to visit Lord Egmont, Poole invited De Quincey to stay on until Coleridge returned. On the first morning he escorted De Quincey on a ride to Alfoxden. The ferny Quantock Hills, as De Quincey called them, delighted him not only in themselves but for their associations with Wordsworth's poetry. They ate a late afternoon dinner at Poole's and talked about Coleridge as they ate, particularly his habit of borrowing phrases from the poetry of others. Two or three days later, Coleridge had not returned.

Lord Egmont's carriage drew up in St Mary Street and its owner came to call on Poole. He brought Coleridge a present that would undoubtedly please him; it was a canister of expensive snuff. Tom Poole had always been a great snuff-taker, and by this time Coleridge equalled or surpassed him. The old lady whose unfavourable memories of Coleridge found their way into Cornelia Crosse's *Red Letter Days* said that Coleridge used up all the snuff in Nether Stowey. Lord Egmont laughed at his own simplicity in expecting to find Coleridge there. He had lent his carriage to Coleridge a few days previously to take him to John Chubb's where Coleridge had proposed staying just one day before returning to Poole's. De Quincey gathered that nobody, nothing, could combat the fatal habit of procrastination that by this time affected every aspect of Coleridge's life so that even the letters he received were left unopened. By this date many of his friends realised that opium had enslaved him. Lord Egmont displayed to De Quincey his unbounded admiration for Coleridge's genius and his anxiety that Coleridge should get down to some huge work like a history of Christianity instead of talking like an angel and writing little. Not one of the three expressed their regret that Coleridge *the poet* had grown silent!

De Quincey gave up waiting in Stowey and rode on one of Poole's horses to Bridgwater after Poole had directed him to John Chubb's quayside house and its arched stone gateway close to the town gaol. In the light of a summer evening De Quincey rode down Fore Street where his eye immediately picked out a large stone gateway on his right, not far from the bridge. At the same time, he recognised from Poole's description the man who stood under the gate contemplating, dreaming, lost in his inner world. At thirty-five he had started to put on weight. His dark hair fell carelessly over his brow and his grey eyes held a strange light as well as dreaminess. He did not notice the interested stare of the young man riding past. De Quincey had got down and called to an ostler at the Castle Inn on the corner of Fore Street to stable his horse, and was approaching John Chubb's gateway with a greeting before Coleridge observed him. Coleridge received him cordially when he made himself known and took him for a walk round the town where all the inhabitants seemed abroad enjoying the warmth and light of that June Sunday evening. De Quincey observed that many Bridgwater people recognised Coleridge and that they saluted him in the most friendly manner. After a tour of the town, during which De Quincey speedily came under the spell of Coleridge's talk, Coleridge invited him back to Chubb's for dinner, conducted him to a sitting-room and rang the bell for refreshments like someone at liberty to regard the house as his own. They sat for two or three hours while the young student listened enthralled to Coleridge's eloquent and persuasive discourse on a wide range of subjects.

The door opened and a woman came into the room. While she stood hesitating whether to go or stay on finding a visitor there, De Quincey noted that she was in her middle thirties, short and plump with features of a commonplace prettiness that had started to fade. With frigid politeness Coleridge made a bare introduction. 'Mrs Coleridge', he said to De Quincey who bowed to her formally and felt some inexplicable embarrassment. Mrs Coleridge withdrew at once. This glimpse of her recalled to De Quincey the scraps of Stowey gossip, half-sympathetic and half-contemptuous, that he had picked up about her jealousy concerning Coleridge's absorption in Dorothy Wordsworth.

A little later he found himself among the guests assembled at the Chubbs' dinner-table. Dinner was a lively occasion enhanced by Coleridge's brilliant talk maintained throughout, but by this time De Quincey sensed that not only was he forcing himself to maintain it but that he was trying to dominate an underlying depression and sadness.

Some time before he took his leave he confided to Coleridge that he had dosed himself with laudanum to alleviate tooth-ache. Coleridge gave him a solemn warning about making a habit of taking potent drugs and went so far as to let him know that he himself had become hopelessly enslaved by opium. (Everyone knows how little this warning benefited De Quincey.)

About ten o'clock De Quincey decided to walk back to Bristol. Probably Coleridge, who styled himself an indifferent horseman, would ride Tom Poole's horse back to Nether Stowey. De Quincey set out refreshed, on his thirty-five mile journey to Hotwells, the white road ribboning before him under the starlit sky of a wonderful summer night. The silence of the night was unbroken, his ears still echoed to the tune of Coleridge's voice, his brain was alive with thoughts and visions created by his recent contact with that rich and imaginative mind. Nevertheless, he realised with sadness that a remorseless decay was already attacking those marvellous faculties. He walked through the village of Huntspill and skirted East Brent, with the dark bulk of Brent Knoll visible on his left in the starlight. A surly dog followed him silently along the top of a park wall. He heard a child crying through an open window and saw the remains of a fair in one small village. He saw no one about, except a man in the village of Cross not far from Cheddar.

De Quincey was a rich young man and, through the intermediary Cottle, made the generous gift of £300 to Coleridge whose genius had so powerfully impressed him. Later in the summer he gallantly escorted Mrs Coleridge and her children all the way by post-chaise from the West Country to Keswick.

That same summer Poole befriended William Baker, a young currier's apprentice who was also a keen amateur naturalist, and gave him the run of his bookshelves. William Baker walked from Bridgwater on several Sundays and found himself at dinner with the Coleridges. He loved listening to Coleridge talking about poetry but felt out of his depth when Coleridge held forth on metaphysical subjects. He found Mrs Coleridge 'a quiet, unaffected, pleasant lady' and felt very sorry for her when Coleridge sorely tried her patience by such vexatious habits as sitting up very late or getting up from bed if suddenly struck by some idea he wished to set down on paper.

CHAPTER 6

COLERIDGE'S FRIEND, JOHN CHESTER

Looking across the red fields near the Castle of Comfort one sees some ivy-covered ruins of red sandstone that were part of the complex called the Stowey Mine of which the most productive part lay in the small hills behind the little Elizabethan manor-house called Dodington Hall. Here John W. Chester, father of Coleridge's friend, lived for many years. In 1786 he was paid for the haulage of timber and stones on behalf of the copper-mine and at one time acted as referee in a mining dispute. Although not actively concerned with mining both he and John may have had some knowledge of it.

Nine or ten children were born to John W. Chester and his wife; the girls included Elizabeth or Bessy, Susan and Julia, the boys John, born in 1765, Thomas (Tom) and Samuel (Sam) all of whom were known to the Coleridges. Mr Chester was a fairly prosperous tenant of the Marquis of Buckingham and farmed the land belonging to Dodington Parsonage in addition to that apper-taining to Dodington Hall. His beautiful house—still a farmhouse —gave ample room to his big family, who must have enjoyed playing games in the Great Hall with its uneven roof-beams of oak supported on angel-corbels, its oak screens, its minstrels' gallery, its plasterwork fireplace adorned with two grotesque caryatids and bearing the date 1581.

By 1795, after her husband's death, Mrs Chester had become tenant of a small Nether Stowey house with a paddock, another piece of the Marquis of Buckingham's property, and several of her

now grown-up children lived with her. John became co-tenant of
a bit of Stowey land that belonged to the Stogursey almshouse. By
1807 when John had left Stowey, his brother Sam rented all this
piece of land. 'What good luck has Sam Chester had?' inquired
Coleridge in a letter to Poole from Germany. No information
about the Chester brothers' Stowey employments seems to exist, but
it is practically certain that John did some farming there. Sharp-
tongued Hazlitt described his countrified corduroy breeches and
stout boots, his hazel-stick pulled out of a hedge, his shambling
drover's walk, and when Chester was in Germany Tom Poole
sent him, through a letter to Coleridge, some solemn advice
about improving his agricultural knowledge. 'It would be a
good object for Chester to take a very accurate account of
agriculture, horticulture, implements, every species of rural management, which he has opportunity of observing.' Chester was
thirty-three years old, the same age as Poole, his well-meaning
mentor.

One cannot say what formal education John Chester ever
received. Poole may have felt sympathy for him because he made
efforts to educate himself; in Germany he made moderate progress
in learning German, and in Stowey he took some French lessons.
Hazlitt made it plain that Chester was in no way qualified to take
part in the discussion of poetry or metaphysics with Coleridge and
that he did not try. He was content to hang in admiration on
every word that fell from Coleridge's lips, incomprehensible as
his friend's discourse was to him. According to Hazlitt he was as
attracted by Coleridge's talk as flies to the honey-pot and turned
his walk into a trot to keep up with Coleridge's stride, listening in
fascination. He hardly opened his own mouth to talk at all during
their long walk to Lynton, except to tell Hazlitt that he thought
Coleridge a wonderful man, but when they picked up a strange
seaweed on the sands, Chester was able to tell his brilliant
companions the country name for it. On the other hand, if John
Chester had been nothing more than an uneducated rustic he
would not have found himself so much in Coleridge's company,
nor would he have been welcomed as an Alfoxden visitor. It seems
likely that he was among the dozen guests at dinner at Alfoxden
in July 1797, and Dorothy Wordsworth's journal recorded that

on 24 March, 1798 Coleridge came to Alfoxden with their friend Ellen Cruickshank and 'the Chesters'.

It is rather surprising that such close friends as the Wordsworths and Coleridge took John Chester on their expedition to Germany, but their written references to his presence never imply that he was an intruder. Coleridge was subsidised by the Wedgwoods but Chester travelled at his own expense, £32 of his money being deposited with Josiah Wedgwood just before Chester left England. From Germany he wrote to his brother in Stowey to send him out £25 and £30 on separate occasions, and Coleridge once borrowed £5 from him.

In Coleridge's first letter to his wife in Stowey, he sent his love to the Chesters, Bessy, Susan and Julia. The latter message was repeated in letters to Poole who was sometimes charged with conveying 'Chester's love and duty to his mother'. When Coleridge and Chester went on alone to Ratzeburg, Tom Poole wrote to Coleridge to express his stern disapproval, telling him to remember that the object of his journey was the acquiring of a perfect knowledge of German and that he ought to live with Germans. 'Beware of being too much with Chester, I could wish you had not both been in 1 house.' Coleridge took no notice of this advice and established a cheerful, affectionate companionship with Chester that was strengthened daily by the sharing of hardships, pleasures, economies. Coleridge enclosed in a letter to Sara one from Chester to his mother who must pay Sara half the postage: 'we save 1s by sending a double letter'.

In several letters he told Sara she must give Chester's 'love and remembrance' to his family. Both men hung anxiously on the arrival of the post—four times weekly—and suffered when letters were lacking. 'No letters from England!' Chester would cry, thus striking a knell, Coleridge said, four times a week. 'Why don't you read the letter?' demanded Chester when Coleridge stood holding one half-stupidly because afraid of reading bad news about his baby son. Coleridge wrote sharp criticism of Chester's family in a letter to Tom Poole because in eight months Chester himself received only a single letter.

The two men kept together, experiencing equal surprise at novel German customs like the supplying of two feather beds apiece, 'one above and one below, instead of bed cloaths'. They were astonished also to find white bread so uncommon that at little German fairs 'twists of white bread' were on sale as a special delight, laid out on trays covered with white napkins, just as gingerbread was on sale in England at little fairs like the September fair in Stowey. Chester was generally included in the invitations Coleridge received to social functions from Germans who inclined to lionise him. One can plainly see Mrs Coleridge pulling down the corners of her mouth when she wrote from Bristol to Tom Poole: 'I am weary of this long absence . . . shocked at the description of jovial parties, their manner and their mirth must be excessively disgusting. I wonder how *Chester* likes them?'

Chester went with Coleridge on the tour through the Harz mountains with a party that included George Bellas Greenough, first president of the Geological Society, sometimes sleeping on straw. At Clausthal, Chester and the others went down one of the mines while Coleridge stayed at home writing to Sara because 'I shall see nothing new after what I had seen at Stowey'.

At the start of a circuitous journey home both Chester and Coleridge were struck by the novel spectacle of a wild boar with an immense cluster of glow-worms round his tail. Chester, however, had acquired a nasty infection. Coleridge wrote a graphic description of the whitlow on his nose, the hideous discoloration of his face. 'Poor Chester, God bless him!' he remarked affectionately. A little later he wrote 'Chester has got St Antony's fire in his legs and his arse is sore'.

The two of them were greatly worried when they reached Cuxhaven because their boxes of clothes had not arrived and neither had Coleridge's box containing the metaphysical books on which he had spent £30. They had hoped to put on clean shirts but evidently travelled home to Stowey in a state of grubbiness.

Did Coleridge ever make any effort to keep in touch with John Chester? It is not very likely when one remembers the terrible change that had come over him by 1807, when he saw Stowey for the last time and by when Chester had left. But over and over again, in letters written from London or Keswick to Tom Poole during 1800 and 1801, Coleridge sent his love, sometimes 'my kind love' to Chester, requested Poole to tell Chester that he would write to him and once that he would write a week later about Chester's German books. He suggested that Chester and Poole should take the *Morning Post* between them as he was contributing articles. Once he told Poole that Mrs Coleridge begged for a letter from Ward, 'a letter full of news, Stowey news, of Mr and Mrs Rich, of the Chesters'. Poole himself good-naturedly wrote to Mrs Coleridge, informing her that the Chesters were 'as usual' and that the girls had neither husbands nor sweethearts. As for John—Poole never praised him warmly—he was taking French lessons from the Abbé Barbey, the French priest exiled in Stowey, and already boasted of his progress although the Abbé told Poole that Chester 'knew little about it'.

The scientist George Bellas Greenough turned up in Nether Stowey in 1801 to visit John Chester who told him all the news of Coleridge, about his leaving Stowey, and working in London. He had told Chester that he would write to Greenough, and some time later Coleridge wrote to Poole to obtain Greenough's address for him from Chester. He did write to Greenough and say that news of the latter's Stowey visit filled him with deep emotion. He blamed his neglect of correspondence on his commitments, not on the fatal inertia that bound him. Chester had told Greenough that Coleridge's Stowey friends never heard from him—that even Tom Poole went long spells without a letter, and that news of Coleridge came only in letters from his wife.

Yet Coleridge retained some affection for the Chesters. He wrote from Keswick to Poole in September 1801 to tell him how greatly Sara had been shocked by news of the death of John's sister Susan. As for Coleridge himself, 'I felt a sort of pain—just enough to bring a tear upon my cheek some 5 minutes after I heard. Poor Mrs Chester!'

Many years later Mrs Coleridge wrote to Poole that 'poor Mrs Chester' would not leave many descendants in spite of her brood of children. A few years earlier Poole had told her that John's brother Tom was dying. Mrs Coleridge kept up the habit of sending her love to Mrs Chester as well as to her daughter Elizabeth who had married a Mr Ridler from Stogursey and made a point of seeing Mrs Ridler when she found herself in Stowey in later years. In 1807, a letter from Tom Poole to John Chester in Cornwall told him of the Coleridges' visit.

When John Chester lived with his parents at Dodington a well-loved visitor was the Quaker Cornishman William Jenkin of Redruth who was steward of the Lanhydrock estates (that included copper-mines). He was also mineral agent to the Marquis of Buckingham who owned copper-mines in Cornwall, and in this capacity he came up to Dodington as adviser to the Marquis's Somerset copper-mine. At the same time he would visit his two little girls, Elizabeth, called Betsy, and Grace at their Quaker School at Milverton not far from Taunton. The Chesters sometimes had Betsy to stay with them when she had a few days' holiday. In 1803 John Chester married Betsy who was twelve years younger than he and had been christened by John Wesley. Four of the six children born to John and Betsy received Chester family names: John, Susan, Julia and Elizabeth who was probably named after her mother rather than Chester's sister. By the time of his marriage Chester held a very responsible post at Tin Croft Mine at Redruth in which he held some shares. He acted as purser, paying out dues and shares and writing reports. By 1805, when John, his first child, was born, he had achieved considerable prosperity, owning shares in another mine called Wheal Ann, shares in coastal vessels sailing from Portreath and shares in a carrying agency that conveyed ore on the backs of mules. Later he owned a farm near Redruth.

Tom Poole met him again when Poole visited William Jenkin in order to look at Cornish mine-machinery, and later consulted Chester about reviving the Stowey copper-mine.

John Chester, his wife and children, were buried in the Friends' Burial Ground at Redruth. His estate included land and timber at Kilton, just a few miles from Stowey.

CHAPTER 7

THE ALFOXDEN YEAR: THE ALFOXDEN JOURNAL (1)

Early in July, 1797, Coleridge fetched the Wordsworths from Dorset in Poole's chaise, jolting them over forty miles of vile roads to be accommodated with Lamb in his crowded cottage. They started immediate exploration of the countryside and Dorothy wrote to Mary Hutchinson—later William's wife—that they were enchanted by the lovely hills, the woods, the sea and clear pebbly brooks, telling her that 'in a wander by ourselves' they had come upon a deep, hidden dell or combe where great trees shaded the steep slopes and a foaming hill-stream broken by a waterfall rushed along the bottom. Immediately they began to search for a small cottage in this beautiful district where they would have the company of the new friend to whom they already felt strongly attached.

Exploring further they found that Dorothy's combe, now called Holford Glen with its waterfall inexplicably smaller than in 1797 and its wealth of trees drastically reduced, lay inside the park boundaries of Alfoxden, the St Albyns' early eighteenth-century house that Dorothy called a mansion. To their pleasure and surprise Tom Poole told them that Alfoxden itself could be rented furnished for only £23 a year, taxes paid. He introduced them to the St Albyns' bailiff John Bartholomew who at that time rented it himself. With his son he occupied Alfoxden Farm and Pardlestone Farm, St Albyn property, that could be reached by following the road through Alfoxden Park, over the hill and down into Pardlestone Lane that runs on to Putsham, part of the parish of

Kilve. This road became a favourite route of the Wordsworths, both for calling on Mr Bartholomew and for reaching Kilve and its shore by the green sea. In winter they sometimes found this way too muddy and turned back.

On 7 July 1797 Bartholomew and Wordsworth signed the agreement, witnessed by Tom Poole, that let Wordsworth the stables, gardens, coach-house, furniture, and Allfoxen House itself—the local pronunciation—for one year from midsummer. The Somerset Record Office still owns the document. Wordsworth and Coleridge often styled the house Allfoxen in their letters although Coleridge dubbed it The Foxes for fun.

Poole vouched for Wordsworth's respectability and Mr Bartholomew thought him a satisfactory tenant. The actual owner of Alfoxden, Langley St Albyn, was a boy of ten, away at a Bristol school called The Fort kept by the Rev Mr Seyer, whose pupils, frequently caned, then included Andrew Crosse of Broomfield (later a friend of Poole and Humphry Davy) and the very rich, generous boy John Kenyon who would live at Woodlands House, Holford, from 1808-1815 when he sometimes visited Poole. Later he became the friend of Southey, Coleridge and Wordsworth. While at Woodlands he absorbed local recollections of the trio which, years afterwards, he passed on to Cornelia Crosse who wrote them down, including the opinion of one stubborn old man: 'They was a bad lot'.

The St Albyn boy had been born a Gravenor, son of a Bristol merchant, and inherited Alfoxden from his maternal grandfather, the Rev Lancelot St Albyn, originally of Nether Stowey, rector of Stringston, and vicar of Wembdon, near Bridgwater. Lancelot's widow had a life interest in the estate and it was to this grandmother that Mr Bartholomew had to account for his choice of tenant. After her death, Langley legally assumed the name of St Albyn. As Alfoxden was then a detached portion of Stringston parish, the St Albyn monuments are in Stringston church, not at Holford. In 1886 Alfoxden was amalgamated with Holford, the village the Wordsworths always regarded as their Somerset address. The main part of Holford contained only thirty houses, mostly thatched cottages, lying in what topographers called 'a romantick winding hollow'—still an appropriate description. They included

Page 143 The Deer Pond, Holford

Page 144 (above) A Quantock hilltop; (below) Ash Farm, Porlock, situated ¼ mile from Culbone church. It is reputed to be the house where Coleridge wrote 'Kubla Khan'

a farmhouse, a shoemaker's, a baker's and a blacksmith's whose forge, near the Plough Inn, was demolished recently to make more space in front of the inn. A light wooden footbridge spanned the stream in the glen and made a convenient short-cut for Dorothy when she walked to the baker's or cobbler's or 'crossed the water with letters' for the carrier. A photograph of Holford Glen taken about 1900 shows a similar bridge.

The Wordsworths moved in on Sunday, 16 July 1797 without returning to Racedown and Dorothy loved Alfoxden from the beginning; 'that dear and beautiful place' she called it when leaving, and Wordsworth himself wrote of its 'enchanting beauty'. The elegant, spacious house with its classical modillioned pediment, Tuscan portico, white walls, and roof of bluish slate looked particularly beautiful in moonlight. Behind it, meadows, wheatfields and pastures interspersed with woodland, extended to the silver line of the Bristol Channel. It faced southward, towards the hills where charcoal burners worked in the oakwood that covered the slopes and where sheep and ponies ran on the open, heathery moorlands above. A high hill rose immediately in front of the house, scattered with great trees and cloaked with fern that, as Dorothy said, made 'couching-places for the slim fawns' they startled on their walks. Red deer from the Quantocks roamed near the house, at night Hazlitt 'heard the loud stag speak' from the park. Owls hooted from the trees, particularly from the great elm, the vast and venerable oak that lifted contorted arms to the sky, and the long-remembered beech that sent huge branches in and out of the ground of the hill-slope near the house so that they looked like coiling serpents. A graceful larch, where the redbreast perched, stood near the front door that opened on a little court with a grass-plot, a gravel walk that William paced when composing verse, and a bed of moss-roses. The house was nearly a century old; probably part of its north side was added some years after the Wordsworths left. It had nine bedrooms, three parlours, a hall, as well as its kitchen, attics and cellars. Two of the parlours have been made into the long panelled room on the right (as one enters). Living rooms and bedrooms were finely proportioned and elegantly furnished. The bedroom Hazlitt slept in on his 1798 visit had blue hangings with St Albyn family portraits on the

I

walls. The lofty parlours had oak panelling and fireplaces adorned by blue and white Dutch tiles displaying sailing ships and windmills. When the Wordsworths dined they looked through long windows at pastoral landscape rimmed by the sea. The parlours were difficult to heat in winter although Dorothy stoked fires with armfuls of wood she had gathered up under the trees of the park. She called the house a mansion, suitable for 'a dozen families like ours'.

Her favourite parlour looked out on the well-stocked kitchen garden, but when she sat writing she occupied a window that gave her a view of the Alfoxden wood, rounded on top like a dome, that had a great grove of hollies growing beneath its trees. A herd of little donkeys liked to shelter under the hollies; she got used to their movements, to the rustle of the shy deer, to the cold crying of the owls when she walked unafraid through the wood at night. Sometimes Coleridge walked with her or William came to meet her. At the bottom of the wood lay their sylvan glen with the rushing brook and waterfall that all of them loved. Birds hopped and played there; in late spring it resounded with the singing of nightingales. The little dye-house, St Albyn property, that was used by the owner of a silk-mill and that has left its ruined walls and wheel in the depths of the glen, may not have been built until after the Wordsworths' departure. On the other hand, its user may have been the 'manufacturer' whose dog Dorothy sometimes heard howling at night.

Coleridge came to stay during their first week and at once they all began roaming the hilltops and combes, by night and day. Before this, Coleridge had wandered alone with his memorandum book. Village people eyed all three with suspicion and bewilderment, staring particularly at the newcomers who spoke in a markedly different way and seemed strange, ill-dressed, impecunious people to live in a great house. The young woman, aged twenty-five, wore old clothes for walking and went out in all weathers. She was tanned dark brown as a gipsy, had brilliant, almost wild grey eyes. Her manner was eager and impetuous and although she liked lonely places she seemed nervous and highly-strung. She lay down on grass or heather, set out at dusk, returned in the dark sometimes with Mr Coldridge from Stowey, and sometimes alone

—both equally questionable forms of behaviour. The man was two years her senior, called himself her brother—which might be doubted—and dressed in out-of-date striped pantaloons and a brown fustian jacket. At times he walked alone, silent, morose, lost in thought, staring at the moon and stars or out at the sea beyond Kilve. Sometimes he muttered to himself, sometimes talked to a passing woodman or shepherd. His face had a curiously worn, severe look for his years, yet occasionally, when walking with his friends, he would break into convulsive laughter that creased deeper the furrows in his cheeks. He and the woman Dorothy seemed always happy to be together. How did he maintain her and himself without working and obviously without a fortune? Thomas Jones who worked as odd-job man at Alfoxden reported that they had very queer habits, even washing and mending their clothes on a Sunday. He didn't like such behaviour and contemplated leaving rather than be mixed-up with such characters. They asked odd questions about the brook and the river Parret at Combwich; they carried camp-stools to sit on during their long walks and noted things down in a portfolio. They had persistently cross-questioned old Christopher Trickey and his wife who lived in a tumbledown cottage in the sloping field opposite the dog pound by Alfoxden gates (the ruined dog pound is still there). Trickey, very poor and feeble by that time, had been a well-known huntsman for the Alfoxden squires in his younger days. Faltering and ignorant, he found questions about the course of the familiar brook by his door almost incomprehensible; he confided his perplexity to Thomas Jones who shook his head at the French people's ways—he was sure they were French, and told Charles Mogg, a former Alfoxden servant returned on a visit, that queer and dangerous people had taken the old place: he felt sure they were spies and had wished himself safely elsewhere on the Sunday, a week after their arrival, when he had had to help wait on a dozen guests invited for three o'clock dinner—several of them very odd customers. He had been particularly frightened by a small, stout man with lank black hair and sickly, sallow face who wore glasses and a white hat and who stood up after dinner to hold forth in a loud ranting manner like a public orator.

This man who scared the simple Jones was no other than

John Thelwall, the notorious Jacobin who had stood trial for treason and been acquitted. All he sought, as he said in a poem he wrote in Bridgwater, was a retired place to live in with his wife and infants. By very bad luck he had turned up uninvited at Coleridge's cottage on Sunday, 16 July, where Sara had started preparing for a huge washday after her guests' departure. She deserted the wash-tub to take him over to Alfoxden for Monday breakfast. He wrote delightedly to his wife of the rambles they had taken that day, in lovely places that included 'the wild romantick dell' where the foaming torrent wound its course. They all went back and forth to Stowey, were a great deal with Tom Poole, walked and talked. On the Sunday, after old Mrs Poole had given the Coleridges a great joint of lamb, they gathered with Poole and others at Alfoxden in glorious weather to hear Wordsworth read his tragedy *The Borderers* that he hoped would be accepted for the London stage. Already Wordsworth felt the warmest respect for Poole without the violent affection shown by Coleridge. Some years after, when he wrote 'Michael' he told Poole in a letter from Grasmere, 'In writing it I had your character often before my eyes and sometimes thought I was delineating such a man as you yourself would have been under the same circumstances'.

Poole brought along to dinner Mr and Mrs John Cruickshank, possibly Thomas Ward, John Chester and his friend Willmott, a former silk throwster of Sherborne dispossessed of his father's silk-mill and farming at Woodlands, which he rented. This efficient, hardworking man was later employed, through Poole's warm recommendation, as bailiff on the Wedgwoods' Dorset estate, yet because of his friendships Charlotte Poole, for one, wrote him down as another politically dangerous person and at the same time recorded her shocked amazement at Thelwall's visits to Cousin Tom and Mr Coldridge.

'To what are we coming?' she wrote.

Thelwall departed. Wordsworth returned to Racedown and fetched four-year-old Basil, the motherless child of his barrister friend Basil Montagu who paid the Wordsworths a modest sum to bring him up and, for part of the Alfoxden year, paid nothing. This child who had been a pale, miserable little creature when they took him, played in joyful freedom at Alfoxden, familiar with trees, stones, birds, animals. He grew hardy and happy and stayed out in all weathers. Generally he played alone, but at times he played with a Holford cottage child whom Dorothy considered very spoiled, and was taken with him to play on the shore at Kilve. That August Basil Montagu senior and a Bristol friend came for a visit that was suspiciously noted by the watchful Thomas Jones. With little Basil, Wordsworth brought from Racedown their dear servant Peggy Marsh, who had just married a Dorset blacksmith but wanted to earn a little money and who in any case, 'would have followed them to the world's end' as Dorothy said. After leaving Alfoxden in 1798 Dorothy wrote to her, sent her parcels and money, for poor Peggy went back to the bitter lot of many women of her class at that time: grinding poverty, a harsh husband, continual childbearing. At Alfoxden she was cheerful and chatty, easily 'picked' for information by Jones when she got him to come weeding. By this time he was receiving extra shillings from a mysterious source.

Charles Mogg visited a woman in the service of Dr Daniel Lysons at Bath. He had known her as the Alfoxden cook. While she entertained him in the Lysons' kitchen he poured out his tale of the doings of the Alfoxden newcomers. The cook told her master who took it seriously enough to pass on the so-called facts to the Duke of Portland at the Home Office. (It must be remembered that England lived on the verge of invasion and that the government feared enemy agents.) Dr Lysons informed the duke that emigrant French people had 'contrived to get possession of a Mansion House at Alfoxden late belonging to the Rev Mr St Albyn', the master had no wife, 'only a woman who passes for his sister', they were 'very attentive to the river', and so on. At once the Home Office despatched an agent called Walsh to interview Mogg at Hungerford where the farrago of nonsense was repeated. After Walsh's report the Home Office ordered him down to Somerset, complete with a few pounds to pay informers, to spy on the suspects without putting them to flight. If Walsh needed assistance he was to apply to a local landowner and magistrate Sir Philip Hales who lived at Brymore, Cannington, a house on the site of the present Brymore School that had belonged to his ancestor John Pym, Cromwell's contemporary. Sir Philip's signature appears often on the Cannington Vestry books in 1797 and 1798 and John Chubb drew a glum-faced portrait of him in his younger days. Perhaps Sir Philip performed only his magisterial duty in the spy affair but Coleridge seems to have regarded 'the titled Dogberry' as a prime instigator and as one of the aristocrats who 'caballed long and loudly even against Wordsworth'. (Lord Somerville of Fitzhead near Taunton was mentioned also.) Coleridge said afterwards that he saw the agent Walsh, whom he nicknamed Bardolph, peering at him and the Wordsworths from behind a rock when they walked by the sea at Kilve and that Walsh joined him along the road trying to inveigle him into conversation. The Wordsworths, however, seem to have been ignorant of Walsh's presence although they could scarcely have been unaware of the local inhabitants' unfriendly stares and muttered remarks. Walsh took a room at the Globe Inn in Castle Street, Nether Stowey on August 15 and was overjoyed that during his first drink a Mr Woodhouse, member of a well-to-do Stowey family, came in to ask Edward Tucker the landlord the latest news of 'those rascals from Alfoxden' and whether Thelwall had left. At that name Walsh's ears pricked up. Tucker and Mr Woodhouse confirmed the fact of Thelwall's visit and told him that the people at Alfoxden were not French but very dangerous Englishmen, a nest of them, headed by a person called Wordsworth. They were friendly with Mr Coldridge who had a printing-press in his house and they were protected by Tom Poole, tanner and a man of property, who held violent, dangerous opinions and headed a Poor Man's Club of 150 members who would obey his commands at any time.

All this was solemnly reported to the Home Office along with various inaccurate or exaggerated statements: the Wordsworths came from Honiton; Tom Poole was surety for their rent; Thelwall was coming to live at Alfoxden; Wordsworth was a smuggler; Wordsworth kept a still to make spirits, it had been smelt; Wordsworth roved the hills 'like a partridge'.

Not surprisingly the whole affair died down for lack of substantial evidence against Wordsworth or Coleridge. Locally Coleridge became accepted. He had an ordinary wife and baby and preached in chapels. The more reticent, self-sufficient Wordsworths were never wholly trusted. The little boy Basil seemed another inexplicable feature of their household. In the end the elderly Mrs St Albyn heard the story, grew angry at Mr Bartholomew's bad choice of tenants for her grandson's house and said that the lease would certainly not be renewed on its expiry in 1798. As early as September 1797 Tom Poole wrote her a respectful letter pointing out what good tenants the Wordsworths made for such a house and that Dr Fisher, a former vicar of Stowey, knew their uncle Canon Cookson, a canon of Windsor like himself.

Mrs St Albyn stuck to her guns. Wordsworth said afterwards that he never asked her to alter her decision and that he left simply because she had let the house to John Cruickshank. It is not certain where she was living. Dorothy Wordsworth recorded that they walked to Crowcombe 'to make the appeal' in April 1798. This cannot be explained as an appeal to Mrs St Albyn, since James Barnard, husband of the Carew heiress, was master of Crowcombe Court at that date. The suggestion that he heard an appeal against their taxes, in his capacity as magistrate, is refuted by the tenancy agreement which states that Mr Bartholomew paid them.

From September onwards the Wordsworths knew that their days at Alfoxden were strictly numbered. They kept the knowledge in the background of their minds and did not let it cloud their year of happiness. Tom Wedgwood and another friend, James Tobin, came from Bristol for a five-day visit in September and found that the memory of all other places temporarily vanished; they felt islanded in some remote Elysium.

On and off the Wordsworths had several people to stay before Christmas. In August Azariah Pinney came, one of the two rich sons of John Pinney of Bristol who owned sugar plantations in the West Indies. The brothers had generously lent Racedown to Wordsworth. John Pinney owned a manorhouse at Somerton, the old capital of Somerset, where the magnificent church contains a monument to him. Coleridge borrowed money from John Pinney on one occasion and may have visited him at Somerton. At the same time as Pinney, Basil Montagu came again to see his little son who figures as Edward in Wordsworth's poems. Seventeen years later Mrs Coleridge wrote to Tom Poole that he must surely remember the little boy he used to see playing at Alfoxden. She had just seen him at Southey's house, a youth fearfully stricken by consumption, being blistered and bled while blood came from his lungs and Dorothy Wordsworth nursed him with the aid of an old servant and remained constantly at his bedside.

Charles Lloyd, Coleridge's former boarder, came for a few days in September and when talking to Dorothy started his malevolent campaign of vilifying Coleridge that in the following spring plunged Coleridge into black melancholy. Basil Montagu came in December to take charge of Basil while William and Dorothy went to London to attempt getting *The Borderers* put on the stage. They failed but went to theatres and saw several plays before returning to the quiet of Alfoxden. Montagu left, carrying a parcel of five beautiful new linen shirts, made by Dorothy, for delivery to Richard Wordsworth, their lawyer brother. He carelessly left it at Coleridge's cottage in Lime Street where it languished till April when Dorothy sent it on with five more shirts. The carrier Milton took it to Bridgwater.

About 20 May young William Hazlitt came. Wordsworth was in Bristol when Coleridge brought Hazlitt from Stowey to stay a night. Dorothy certainly never heeded the conventions that hemmed in the young women of her day for she entertained both men to a supper Hazlitt called frugal and put them up for the night. After breakfast they sat on the trunk of a fallen ash in the Alfoxden park while Coleridge, in the voice Hazlitt recalled years later for its music and sonority, read aloud William's recently-written poems, 'The Thorn', 'The Mad Mother', 'The Idiot Boy', 'The Complaint of a Forsaken Indian Woman'. The experience of hearing these made Hazlitt aware of a new spirit in poetry: he compared its effect to that made by turning up fresh soil or by the first breath of spring. He continued to feel spellbound by Coleridge's voice when they walked back to Stowey that night between the great, full-foliaged oaks of the wood and past the stream and white waterfall that gleamed in the summer moonlight. He met Wordsworth late the following evening when Wordsworth arrived in Stowey from Bristol. At first sight Hazlitt compared him to Don Quixote, he was so gaunt and wore such old-fashioned clothes, but within a few minutes he was impressed by the stern and thoughtful brow, the penetrating, almost fiery glance, the mouth bracketed by furrows laughter had ploughed. Wordsworth's voice too, different as it was from Coleridge's, made a permanent impression, gushing freely as a mountain-stream once he began to talk, and tinctured with a north-country pronunciation 'like the crust on wine'. He told them of his visit to the theatre in Bristol and then looked through the parlour lattice to comment on the sunset light. His walk had famished him and he made inroads into Sara Coleridge's Cheshire cheese. (Sometimes Tom Poole procured his friends fine Somerset cheese from his uncle in Taunton, but at Alfoxden Dorothy wrote off for a Sockburn cheese to be sent from the north.)

Next day Wordsworth read 'Peter Bell' aloud to Coleridge and Hazlitt, again in the open air at Alfoxden. Within the next fortnight Wordsworth wrote two poems, 'The Tables Turned' and 'Expostulation and Reply' which grew directly from his conversation with Hazlitt. In early June they walked to Lynton with Coleridge and John Chester.

Joseph Cottle paid a visit in May that must have overlapped Hazlitt's although in their own accounts of visits to Alfoxden they did not mention each other. Wordsworth had continually pressed Cottle to come during that tardy but glorious spring, telling him that daily the country round Alfoxden grew more beautiful, that he had written many new poems and wished to read them to Cottle under the old trees of the park. So Cottle came in late May, making a journey that caused hilarity on the day and later, whenever any of them remembered it. Did Cottle exaggerate the farcical happenings of that lovely day in May when years later he wrote his description of driving Wordsworth in a gig from Bristol along the dusty roads, between hedges and banks rich with the wild flowers of May, towards Nether Stowey? Here they picked up Coleridge and Dorothy in Lime Street, leaving Mrs Coleridge at home with her new baby Berkeley born that month. They had given a few pence to a wayside tramp—a sturdy *rat* of a beggar, Cottle angrily described him—during a break when they stood cloud-gazing. On their arrival in the Alfoxden courtyard they found he had smelt out and stolen the large piece of cheese on which, with a brown loaf, lettuces from the Alfoxden garden and a bottle of brandy, they had meant to dine. Unbuckling the horse Coleridge cheerfully declared that the brandy would turn the bread and lettuce into a feast. He let the shafts of the gig drop too smartly and sent the brandy-bottle rolling from the gig to smash on the stones of the yard. Neither Coleridge nor Wordsworth could pull the horse's leather collar over its head. Coleridge sweated vainly over the task, declaring that the horse's head must have grown—gout perhaps. 'La! master, do it like this!' said competent Peggy Marsh, suddenly appearing at the horse's head and skilfully reversing the collar to slip it off with ease. At last they sat down at the Alfoxden table, ruefully surveying the empty cheese dish before falling-to on brown bread and cos lettuce, washed down with cold water. Immediately they found that Peggy was 'out' of salt. But all of them laughed as they munched their way through dinner. Provisions bought in Holford that afternoon made them a better supper.

Wordsworth now persuaded Cottle to publish his poems with Coleridge's 'Ancient Mariner' in a single volume to be entitled *Lyrical Ballads*. Wordsworth insisted on joint publication for he and Coleridge had cherished the plan to combine in producing a volume of poems ever since the cloudy November day when they walked to Watchet. On his departure, therefore, Cottle carried away the manuscripts of Wordsworth's Alfoxden poems and the 'Ancient Mariner'. He paid 30 guineas for the copyright.

Before he left they took Cottle on their long, familiar walk to Lynton and the Valley of the Rocks by way of Porlock and Culbone, seeing Exmoor in the full glory of springtime weather.

Their local visitors were not numerous. Coleridge, of course, came almost daily, stayed as long as he wished, remained overnight and from 9 March to 18 March, stayed there with his wife and Hartley. He and Wordsworth wrote at the same table. Tom Poole rode over fairly often and sometimes stayed to dinner or drank tea in the parlour, but he was too busy a man to spend long hours with them except at his own house. Now and again John Chester came from Stowey, bringing some of his family—perhaps a sister, Susan or Julia. John Cruickshank and his wife Anna came occasionally, and once or twice his sister Ellen. Mr Bartholomew from

Alfoxden Farm sometimes looked in and must have felt relieved to observe that at least his so-called unsatisfactory tenants kept the house and furniture cleaned and undamaged, just as Tom Poole had pointed out to Mrs St Albyn who, however, firmly gave her tenants the agreed three-months' notice in March 1798.

In spite of the hours spent on long walks and reading, Dorothy Wordsworth was a domesticated woman although never so enslaved by housework that a lovely day failed to make her put it aside and go out. Her *Grasmere Journal* 1800-1803 is much longer and more detailed than the *Alfoxden Journal*—and so, except from a purely Somerset standpoint, much more interesting —and it gives many particulars of domestic tasks she undertook while Molly Fisher, like Peggy at Alfoxden 'our dear, good Peggy' did the rougher chores. The making of bread, tarts, puddings, roasting a goose, making gooseberry jam, mending clothes, binding carpets, making curtains, washing and ironing are among the jobs frequently performed. It is reasonable to believe that she was as good a housewife at Alfoxden even though she mentions nothing about domestic tasks except washing, starching and hanging out linen and, in her letters, the making of her brother Richard's shirts, with great care, from the linen of which he and William between them had bought 100 yards several months before she came to Alfoxden. No doubt she made William's shirts as well.

Certainly Alfoxden never seemed their home in the sense Dove Cottage did as, from the start, the seal of impermanence had been put on their stay. Perhaps for that reason she makes no mention of ever gardening at Alfoxden either alone or with William, while the *Grasmere Journal* abounds in references to the sowing and sticking of peas and beans, to planting lilies and London Pride, to bringing home wild flowers like 'Lockety goldings' to set in the border, to accepting columbine plants over somebody's garden wall, to bringing home lemon thyme and planting it by moonlight.

It may safely be assumed that no Holford inhabitant ever offered plants over a cottage gate when Dorothy passed nor sent her a basket of plums in return for a basket of French beans— common happenings at Grasmere—any more than he invited Dorothy and William to drink tea, to play cards after supper, to come in to the fire on a snowy day and put straw in their wet shoes. No such thing is set down in the *Alfoxden Journal*. Nor did the Wordsworths visit any house on the day of a funeral, nor attend a christening, take a look at any small festivity such as the fair at Nether Stowey or even one of the little 'revels' (as they were called until a date well-on in the present century) held at the season of whortleberry-picking at, among other places in the Quantocks, the Castle of Comfort inn with which they were so familiar (Dorothy's letters cover appropriate dates if the journal does not). The *Grasmere Journal* records interest and participation in such things, as well as church-going, not very long after the Wordsworths' arrival. By reason of their birthplace they were, of course, 'home at Grasmere' as they could never be in the south. Their speech and manners did not strike Grasmere people as foreign, no taint of the absurd 'spy' scandal clung to them there, and they did not live isolated in a large house in parkland. Nevertheless, when one remembers that the 1802 census numbered the population of Holford at 113, it is astonishing that the Wordsworths made contact with none of them. Dorothy often saw the blacksmith, the baker, the shoemaker; on a fine day she passed mothers walking with their children, and young girls wearing pink and blue petticoats; on the hills she encountered the woodman with his loaded pony coming along a faintly-marked track, an old man cutting furze, a farm-labourer looking jaunty because it was Sunday. One frosty winter evening, along the road to Stowey, she met a razor-grinder, with a knapsack on his back and wearing a soldier's old red jacket, who had a boy with him to drag his wheel. Yet of these she left not a single lifelike, vivid miniature such as those with which the *Grasmere Journal* is coloured, no mention of their speech, their way of life, their vicissitudes.

William, however, took a penetrating look at them. While not on friendly terms with more prosperous householders he sometimes talked with Christopher Trickey, the old huntsman, outside his cottage on the common, with men who ran a small flock on the hills, sometimes with a passing vagrant or a soldier discharged from the French wars, even with some wild-eyed draggled woman who crazily haunted a stretch of the hills—Coleridge in his notebook mentioned seeing such a one 'under woodland boughs'. Most of all, he liked listening to any old inhabitant who would relate some curious tale of village life, some rustic event that had passed into the annals of the poor.

The *Alfoxden Journal*, apart from its catalogue of day-to-day occupations, abounds in pictures not of people but of landscape, seascape, skyscape. Dorothy lived almost constantly in the company of two poets and often looked on the same things at the same time as they, but the vision with which she looked was peculiarly her own, and a poetic one as much as theirs, characterised by truth and a striking clarity. The night-sky where a continuous thin white cloud parted to reveal the moon sailing in a blue-black vault amid a multitude of stars; a night-sky with a star inside a lunar rainbow; the sky on a windy, cloudy, moonlit night when the heavens seemed in one perpetual motion; a sober grey sea darkly striped by grey clouds; a bluer sea whereon the clouds streaked colour; the sea obscured by vapour that parted to reveal the islands Flat Holm and Steep Holm; the sea brimful as a basin; the sea white under the moon with bright Venus hanging low—how many minute and exquisite pictures her pen created, evening after evening as she sat with her small notebook and quill pen by the wood-fire, scribbling her observations for only William's eye to read. Sometimes the fire was out and she was dead tired after the four-mile walk back from Stowey, more than ready for bed: to please William she generally wrote *something*, however brief. Her delight in the Somerset landscape, however, in all its moods, at any season, produced long paragraphs of such spontaneous artistry that they resemble delicately vivid water-colours: fields of young green wheat streaked with silver lines of water and green hills channelled by streams after rain, with sheep on the slopes; winter trees like black skeletons, the ground beneath them strewn with red holly-berries; the heath on a Quantock hilltop spread with the lace of spiders' gossamers; the bare branches of the oakwood thickened by snow with green moss on the tree-roots and birds on the moss; the hollies of the Alfoxden grove scarlet with berries, green with leaves, burdened with snow; and—fullest landscape of all—the farmhouses of Kilve, Stringston, East and West Quantoxhead, standing with fresh straw at their doors among mossy orchards, fields with haystacks, meadows full of lambs, brown ploughland misted green by springing wheat.

Detail is exquisite: for example, the white heads of snowdrops 'ribbed with green'; the 'thick legs, large heads, black staring eyes' of young lambs; 'our faint shadow going before us' on a bright moonlight night; moss-cups 'proper for fairy goblets'; a beautiful evening, 'very starry, the horned moon'.

The ear too can fancy itself delighted as one reads the journal, catching such sounds as the soothing tinkle of a sheep-bell in the combe, the patter of hail mingled with the scutter of dry leaves, the roaring of the wood in a great wind, the robin's slender song, and over and over again the sound of water—the running of streams down hillside and lane, the voice of the waterfall. 'She gave me eyes, she gave me ears', her brother acknowledged, and a number of his poems prove it.

Dorothy demanded no life of her own. Her existence was bounded by the needs and demands of her brother for whom she kept house, transcribed pages of poetry, wrote letters, read aloud, listened attentively to the reading of his work and whom she fortified with continual encouragement. They were closely and remarkably united—too much so as has been established, although during the Alfoxden year Dorothy did not feel the neurotic attachment that she developed soon after their separation from Coleridge and the start of Coleridge's love-affair with Sara Hutchinson, nor was she plagued by the nervous headaches and ailments that later beset her. At Alfoxden, however, her world, as well as William's, expanded to take in Coleridge so that they did indeed almost become 'three people but one soul' as, it is alleged, Coleridge sentimentally expressed it. They met daily, walking four miles to or from Stowey, along the high road (our A39) or over the hills and along old lanes. They walked miles nearly every day, sometimes two of them, sometimes three, learning the combes, the moorland, the red earth-tracks, and the web of green sheep-paths like the backs of their hands, although they remained curiously hazy about place-names. Dorothy never names a combe or a hill near Holford although Poole and John Bartholomew must have used such familiar names as Hare Knap, Danesborough or Dowsborough, Hodder's Combe, and so on. She names no villages apart from Kilve, Holford, Stowey, and carelessly wrote Crowcombe down as Crookham and the hamlet Putsham as Potsdam.

In one another's company they read and discussed poetry, sauntered in the park, sat down in the sunshine on fallen trees, lay down on the turf on the hills and gazed on the same prospect to which the imagination of Coleridge and Wordsworth responded in such different ways, walked over the fields to Woodlands or down Pardlestone Lane to Kilve, idled in the glen watching the waterfall, returned through the owl-haunted wood in darkness. It was surely inevitable that Dorothy, young and sexually inexperienced for her twenty-six years as well as so exquisitely sensitive to natural beauty and to poetry, should fall in love with Coleridge who was her own age, a poet, a man richly endowed with the power of attraction—as so many acknowledged—and with the most eloquent tongue and musical voice, often crazily gay and boyish, at times melancholy and demanding sympathy. When the two of them walked through the dark wood under a vault of stars or lingered in the wooded glen listening to the nightingales singing in the May moonlight, Coleridge's personality worked its magic: the *Grasmere Journal* has sentences that reveal her love for him although her feeling remained concealed and was perhaps hardly acknowledged even to herself, during the Alfoxden time, for one of her outstanding traits was a naïve innocence. And Coleridge? There is no evidence that he seriously fell in love with her, much as he delighted in her company. But both of them always remembered the twelve-month association as an idyllic experience.

For Wordsworth the Alfoxden year was crucial. The most important factor in the setting of his poetic development on a definite and decided course was Coleridge's friendship. From Coleridge he received criticism that he could trust since it came from a brilliant critical mind as well as from a fellow poet, and an encouragement less likely to be biased than an adoring sister's. The encouragement was powerful enough. Even generous. Tom Poole accused Coleridge of 'prostration' to Wordsworth for Coleridge acclaimed him a giant, the greatest English poet since Milton, long before Wordsworth had produced his finest work.

In later life Coleridge reminded Poole how right he had been.

During his first months at Alfoxden Wordsworth wrote comparatively little. He was walking, looking, listening, meditating on what he had seen and heard and making his own interpretation. By the end of 1797, besides publishing one or two minor poems in the *Morning Post*, he had worked at, and continued his long poem 'The Ruined Cottage' that he had begun at Racedown and would not finish till February. (This later became Book I of his very long poem 'The Excursion'.) He finished 'The Old Cumberland Beggar', a poem also started at Racedown and significant in that it shows Wordsworth beginning to recollect experiences of his boyhood. He revised 'Animal Tranquillity and Decay' (Old Man Travelling) and after his London visit in December wrote the ballad called 'The Reverie of Poor Susan'. In the New Year he wrote 'Goody Blake', 'A Night Piece', 'The Discharged Soldier' (later incorporated in his magnificent autobiographical 'Prelude') and in March 'To My Sister (Lines written at a small distance from my House)', the exquisite 'Lines Written in Early Spring', 'Anecdote for Fathers', 'Simon Lee', 'We are Seven', 'A Whirlblast from behind the Hill', 'The Last of the Flock', 'The Idiot Boy'.

In March of 1798, the hedges and trees remained black and leafless, except for the 'palms' of willow, but in April spring broke over the landscape like a green and rushing wave. 'Within four days the season has advanced with greater rapidity than I ever remember and the country becomes almost every hour more lovely', wrote Wordsworth to Cottle. His poetic genius flowered with the same impetuous haste so that at very short intervals he wrote 'The Thorn', 'Her Eyes are Wild', his long 'Peter Bell', 'Andrew Jones', 'I love upon a stormy night', 'The Complaint of a Forsaken Indian Woman', 'Expostulation and Reply', 'The Tables Turned'. The Alfoxden poetry comprised all his poems published in the 1798 edition of *Lyrical Ballads* and many of the 1805 edition as well—with the exception that only about a fortnight after leaving Somerset he wrote his finest contribution to the 1798 edition which was also one of the greatest and most significant poems he ever wrote—'Lines written a Few Miles above Tintern Abbey'. These poems, as Hazlitt said, turned new soil and blew a different air.

In addition to all this, Wordsworth put the finishing touches to 'Salisbury Plain (Guilt and Sorrow)' and wrote the poem 'A Somersetshire Tragedy' that no longer exists. And early in 1798, in what is known as his *Alfoxden Note-book*, he wrote the agonised lyric 'Away, away, it is the air' that he neither published nor showed his friends. It was the cry of a forbidden passion that he most ruthlessly suppressed.

In April Wordsworth went over to Stowey to have his portrait painted by William Shuter, an obscure artist travelling round in search of commissions. There could not have been many sittings as Shuter apparently did not come to Alfoxden with Coleridge on the following Sunday as expected. His portrait shows a youthful-looking Wordsworth with a raggedly-cut fringe. It was sent by Coleridge to Cottle and is now at Cornell University, USA. Shuter painted Coleridge too. This portrait went to Poole's grand-niece.

Dorothy, unfortunately, left only bare notes of two expeditions to Cheddar that she, William, and Coleridge made during the third week of May. On the first occasion they slept at Bridgwater, on the second at Cross, a Mendip hamlet off the turnpike road to Bristol. Other travellers recorded that Cross possessed 'three capital inns'. After the night at Cross, William went on alone to Bristol while the other two walked back to Stowey where a day or so later he and Cottle picked them up in Cottle's gig.

They left Alfoxden on 26 June with the greatest regret but knew they were not losing, at least for a while, one of the chief attractions it had held for them, the society of Coleridge, since the German tour with him lay ahead. Wordsworth himself had come to a turning-point. His destiny as a poet had been determined by the year at Alfoxden in the company of Dorothy and Coleridge. He had recovered from the crisis of despair caused by his disillusionment concerning the French Revolution and had cast off the load of guilt he had borne since his enforced desertion of Annette Vallon and their child. He left Alfoxden happy and self-confident. Like Coleridge and Dorothy, he never again lived through such an unclouded year.

After a week at Coleridge's cottage they left several boxes of possessions in store with Mrs Coleridge, who could not have had much room for them, and then left Mrs Coleridge herself, for the

German tour. Anxiety about these goods made Wordsworth write from Germany to trouble Poole 'to remove those boxes of ours from that damp room at Mr Coleridge's'. In Bristol Dorothy wrote a letter from Cottle's house in Wine Street with the noise of wheeled traffic in her ears, and told her aunt that the noise jarred her after 'the sweet sounds of Alfoxden', a place that had made her hate cities.

She never saw 'that dear and beautiful place' again. From Germany Wordsworth wrote to Poole that he would return to Alfoxden if it were ever available. He had turned seventy when he paid what he called a farewell visit. In 1841 he travelled to Bath with his wife, the former Mary Hutchinson, to stay with their great friend and Wordsworth's devoted admirer Isabella Fenwick in the house she had taken on North Parade. It is the present Grosvenor Hotel which bears a plaque announcing 'William Wordsworth dwelt here', and has, incidentally, a Wordsworth Bar. In Bath they were entertained by Miss Fenwick's sister and her husband, a Mr Popham from Bagborough in the Quantocks, near Taunton. The chief reason for the visit, although Mrs Wordsworth took the baths and enjoyed the Pophams' dinners, was the long-deferred marriage of their daughter Dora to Mr Quillinan, a Catholic widower, in the Anglican church of St James, destroyed by twentieth-century bombing. The present Woolworth store stands on the site. The marriage certificate states that Edward Quillinan and Dorothy, daughter 'of William Wordsworth gentleman' were married according to the rites of the Anglican church by the Rev John Wordsworth with William Wordsworth junr, one of the witnesses.

Wordsworth felt too unwell to attend at the church. Next day he, his wife, his son and Miss Fenwick drove from Bath, slept at Wells and went on to Ashcott, a village on the Polden Hills and near the peat-moors, to join the newly-married pair for breakfast at Piper's Inn. Afterwards they all made their way to Alfoxden, walking round Wordsworth's youthful haunts, the park, the glen, the hill facing the front entrance. The inevitable changes made during forty-three years saddened Wordsworth greatly. With his wife, his son and Miss Fenwick he spent a few days at Bagborough afterwards.

Cornelia Crosse did not like the changes either when in 1851 she drove from Fyne Court at Broomfield with her elderly husband Andrew Crosse over the hills to Holford by way of very boggy roads leading from the crossroads near the present garage called The Pynes situated on Buncombe Hill above Enmore. The road leads to Nether Stowey where, passing through, she judged Coleridge's former cottage 'mean and unlovely, too dear at £7 a year'. She was a great lover of Coleridge's and Wordsworth's poetry and a very intelligent woman in spite of the somewhat gushing style she used in her memoir to refer to 'sacred places', 'the sacred lime-tree bower was a kind of rough summer-house in Tom Poole's garden'. The prospect of visiting Alfoxden and of dining with the squire Mr St Albyn who had been the juvenile owner Langley in Wordsworth's time, excited her: she had a score of questions to ask him over the dinner-table. She was dis-illusioned. As she said, Squire St Albyn proved to have no more interest in poetry and poets than ever George II had in 'Boetry and Bainting'. Good-natured, but bored, he promised to show her the 'sacred spots' on which she was so well-informed and escorted her round the grounds and common in afternoon sunshine. He could not, however, recall anything about Wordsworth except that as a boy he had seen him 'mooning about the hills'. He was sorry that his 'pig-headed trustees' had insisted on giving Wordsworth notice to leave as the house stood empty afterwards.

Mr Wordsworth, he added, had proved a good and careful tenant.

In the last book of the *Prelude* Wordsworth paid tribute to the unforgettable summer of his youth when, in the company of his sister and of the friend who

> 'in delicious words with happy heart,
> Didst speak the Vision of that Ancient Man,
> The bright-eyed Mariner,'

he himself went

> 'on Quantock's grassy Hills
> Far ranging, and among the sylvan Coombs.'

CHAPTER 8

THE ALFOXDEN JOURNAL (2):
POEMS, PLACES, WALKS

It is a fascinating employment to pick out the impressions and influence of Somerset places and scenes in the poems Wordsworth wrote at Alfoxden and in those Coleridge wrote during his Stowey period—where they are fewer—as well as in several poems written afterwards. The fascination increases as the reader finds poems reflecting, as if in a mirror, the images so clearly defined in Dorothy's *Alfoxden Journal* of which only the entries 20 January 1798—22 May were ever transcribed by its earliest editor in 1897, the manuscript being by great misfortune lost soon after he had used it. It is possible that these were the only entries.

'A Night Piece'—which Wordsworth said he composed extempore on the road—reflects the night of wind, rain and veiled moonlight when William and Dorothy saw the wet shimmer of the road—'semblance of another stream'—between Holford and the Castle of Comfort inn under a sky full of hurrying cloud. The same glittering road, the hedgerow hawthorns carrying sparkling drops on every black spike, the hollies shining in moonlight, reappear in Book IV of the *Prelude*, while the discharged soldier in his faded red coat encountered on a frosty afternoon near the Castle of Comfort makes a brief appearance in the same *Prelude* passage and in the 'Ruined Cottage'. The hill-sheep Dorothy noticed leaving tufts of wool and red marks on palings they had rubbed clean of moss, leave red stains of ruddle on cornerstones of the ruined cottage. Along this same road Wordsworth met, as he tells in 'The Last of the Flock', a Holford villager who had laboured to increase his flock from twenty sheep to fifty that he grazed on the hills until he fell on evil times and, because of the cruel regulations for receiving parish relief, had to sell them one by one to keep his family; he wept over the last lamb he was carrying down to sell, 'close to Alfoxden' Wordsworth said.

In 'Simon Lee the Old Huntsman' Wordsworth names Cardiganshire as the home of the ancient, bent, one-eyed, poverty-stricken man living near the untenanted Ivor Hall of his dead masters, but the old fellow he helped dig up a stump of rotten wood was Christopher Trickey who had babbled to the government agent about the odd strangers at Alfoxden. Renowned a long time for his fleetness of foot and his sounding of the horn, he had been huntsman for St Albyns who hunted with the Quantock staghounds, and the chiming voices of hounds were still a joy to his ears. 'I dearly love their voice' was what he actually said to Wordsworth, stated the latter in 1841 remembering their talks of nearly forty-five years back. Christopher Trickey, who had once afforded to rent a piece of land in Kilve (called Whitehall), built a poor wattle-and-daub cottage on a scrap of ground enclosed from the common at Holford (which is called the Bowling Green today) and cultivated his plot until he became too feeble. The site is now lost in the field sloping down to the stream near the ruined dog pound. Trickey certainly died in poverty, after receiving poor relief from the parish of Cothelstone where he ended his days. In 1841 Wordsworth saw empty ground where the cottage had stood but the old man's figure rose clearly before his eyes and his words echoed in Wordsworth's ears. In 1851 Cornelia Crosse persuaded Squire St Albyn to show her where 'Simon Lee' once lived and was greatly disappointed that the humble dwelling had vanished. This poem and 'The Last of the Flock' illustrate the condition of the rural poor in Somerset at the close of the eighteenth century. Some lines of the 'Old Cumberland Beggar', (later omitted) declare that the destitute old villager must not be deemed more useless than the portly squire in his coach. This belief Wordsworth certainly applied to Christopher Trickey and the Holford shepherd.

Everyone familiar with the Quantocks knows that hardly any

trees grow on the open heath except hollies and the many ancient hawthorns that are snow-white in spring, bare and black in winter, tortured in shape and permanently bent sideways by the sea-wind. The very oldest thorn-trees stay flowerless and skeleton-like all the year, but are overgrown with lichens 'like a stone'. In a later version of his 'Goody Blake' Wordsworth set her home on the side of a hill where sea-blasts made the hawthorns lean sideways. On a stormy day, 19 March 1798, he was struck by the appearance of a stark, lichened thorn-tree silhouetted on the ridge of a hill in the Quantocks and immediately composed his ballad 'The Thorn'. The tragic crazed woman in a red cloak who sat beneath the thorn in all weathers, even when the wind 'cuts like a scythe', rocking herself and wailing, had beside her a heap of moss that covered a mound resembling a baby's grave and the moss-cups made a pattern of brilliant colours, green, vermilion, pearly-white, like those mosses Dorothy described in her journal and which are part of the hilltop vegetation.

In 'Ruth', written in Germany, Wordsworth portrays another crazed village girl who, deserted by her seducer, roamed the Quantocks, sleeping in a barn in winter and under 'a greenwood tree' in summer, near 'the banks of Tone'. The Tone, Taunton's river, does not flow through the Quantocks but Wordsworth found the name convenient for rhyme and not out-of-place in his poetic rendering of some old Quantock tale about a crazy girl who set little watermills in the streams and whose hemlock-flute the Quantock woodman heard on his way home from work. It will be remembered that Coleridge's notebook contains a jotting about the woman 'maniac' who heedlessly crossed the woodman's path in the woods where the boughs swung back and hit her. The woodman Dorothy notices with his laden pony on a Quantock track reappears in 'The Idiot Boy', even the pony with a load of faggots; indeed this ballad, that has often earned ridicule, abounds in references to sights and sounds familiar to Wordsworth during his Holford sojourn. The 'down' covered in fern and gorse, overlooking a wide prospect, is a Quantock hill and the 'long town' Johnny reached after riding for the doctor could be Nether Stowey with its long street. As for the sounds that were audible all that 'long blue night', they were those frequently heard near Alfoxden and in the verses seem like echoes from the journal: the thundering waterfall, the soft-sounding stream, the tremulous night-long crying of the owls. Wordsworth composed this ballad quite gleefully in the shelter of Alfoxden woods and never needed to correct a word. He was started-off by Tom Poole's description of a village idiot boy who declared that when 'the sun shone cold' at night the cocks cried 'tu-whoo!'.

On a mild March morning Wordsworth wrote his verses 'To My Sister' at a small distance from the front of the house and put them in little Basil Montagu's hand to take to Dorothy whom they summoned 'to feel the sun' instead of working indoors. In the poem he called the boy by the name Edward just as in 'Anecdote for Fathers' in which he describes him as a fair, fresh, active boy of five years. So Dorothy too described him in a letter, but at greater length. That morning when Basil ran in with the poem in his hand the robin whose song Dorothy always mentioned with such pleasure in her journal was singing in the tall larch near the door. In 1841 Wordsworth felt disappointed that the tree had not grown to more impressive size. Cornelia Crosse was pleased when Langley St Albyn pointed it out in 1851 and upset to find it cut down a few years later. She never had sight of the huge, coiling, serpentine beech that Wordsworth found so remarkable a feature of the grounds at Alfoxden and that had one great bough torn off by the wind before he left. In 1841 he himself could barely find the spot where it once grew. In 'Anecdote for Fathers', Edward's home is Liswyn Farm: the name came to Wordsworth's mind because Thelwall had taken a farm at Liswen in Wales. A gilded weather-cock, similar to the Alfoxden vane, glitters on the roof of a house surrounded by 'woods and green hills warm' yet the boy prefers his home of a year before, 'Kilve by the green sea', 'Kilve's delightful shore' which lies two or three miles from Alfoxden. 'Smooth shore' is a false description of the loose shingle at Kilve unless 'smooth' refers to the stones planed smooth by the sea. Basil had found it an enjoyable playground.

'Lines Written in Early Spring' is the most spontaneous lyric Wordsworth wrote at Alfoxden. The breath of April seems to blow through it. He composed it in Holford Glen, the 'dell' so often mentioned in Dorothy's journal, that was always green with moss and brambles and backed by many more oaks than now, 'unbranching oaks' Dorothy called them. 'It was a chosen resort of mine', said Wordsworth years later. That day he sat by the brook that runs down through Holford Combe to fall over a stone shelf in a cascade just inside the glen. It flows across fields to the sea at Kilve, after uniting in the glen with the other hill-stream that flows down the slope of Christopher Trickey's cottage-site and past Alfoxden gates. The streams' meeting-place was called the Mare's Pool. When the Wordsworths and Coleridge walked in the glen a slender fallen ash-tree bridged the pool below the waterfall and sent up in a vertical direction its boughs covered with foliage, whitened by the shade, while tresses of ivy swung beneath it. Not surprisingly this ash had disappeared when Wordsworth came in 1841. The little poem paints budding twigs, the periwinkles and primroses that on 12 April Dorothy catalogued with dog-violets and stitchwort. All of them grow there now, the periwinkles trailing over the wall, and it is still low, damp, green with hart's tongue fern (she called it adder's tongue) and filled with the sound of water. Entry is forbidden; the silk-mill ruins are unsafe, and in any case numerous picnickers would not enhance its attractions. In 1841 Wordsworth told Mr St Albyn— whom apparently he encountered—that he wished he would make a narrow path 'for persons who love such scenes to creep along'.

Cornelia Crosse paid a later visit than the one she made in 1851 and was disgusted that her earlier impression of 'the sacred spot' was ruined by the ruthless felling of oaks in the glen and by the building of cottages inside it.

The holly-grove protected by the Alfoxden wood through which the Wordsworths walked to Holford was a place both of them particularly loved, like the glen. In 1841 Wordsworth rejoiced to find it 'in unimpaired beauty', and today it still flourishes, yielding a wonderful harvest for the Christmas market. Dorothy wrote of its beauty after snowfall, of seeing the donkeys shelter there 'in quietness' from a roaring wind, of the sheen of the holly-leaves after rain, and of taking refuge there with William on 18 March when a violent hail-shower came on as they returned home from Stowey so that all the withered oak-leaves strewing the wood 'danced with the hailstones'. William composed a gay little poem on the spot, his 'A Whirlblast from behind the Hill' that tells of the rushing wind, the showering hailstones, the evergreen bower, the towering leafless oaks and their dry fallen leaves agitated in the force of the hail to skip and hop.

In Germany Wordsworth wrote 'The Danish Boy' in which some readers may catch echoes of Quantock legend. The highest hill in the Quantocks, after Will's Neck, is called Danesborough, a variant of its older name Dowsborough; both names are still in use. In spite of the name Danesborough the hill has no associations with the Danes, but local tradition tells of a Danish coastal raid when most of raiders were killed except one flaxen-haired boy hidden by a woman who loved him. His ghost is supposed to haunt Danesborough slopes, softly singing as he wanders. Wordsworth wrote:

> Of flocks upon the neighbouring hills
> He is the darling and the joy;
> And often when no cause appears
> The mountain-ponies prick their ears—
> They hear the Danish boy,
> While in the dell he sits along
> Beside the tree and corner-stone.

Dorothy recorded that on 26 February a clear, beautiful afternoon, they walked to the top of a high hill to see a fortification, and in all probability this refers to the iron-age camp on the summit of Danesborough from which one views a prospect of sea stretching to the cliffs of Wales, as she describes. It made a wonderful look-out over the Severn Sea for the few Roman soldiers stationed there in summer. Wordsworth with his sister and Coleridge, or sometimes Dorothy by herself, often used the stony water-hollowed paths twisting through the coppice oaks on Danesborough's flanks. On a walk back from Stowey they may have turned up the Coach Road by the Counting House (the names still used), passed by the site of Walford's Gibbet and then turned to the right along the broad ride called Danesborough Ditch, before they climbed the flank of the hill to drop down into Butterfly Combe. On 26 February they started from Holford in the afternoon, escorting Coleridge home after dinner and sitting a long time on Danesborough's summit 'to feed upon the prospect . . . magnificent', so that Venus, Jupiter and the moon were shining through the dusk as they descended. The prehistoric camp remains as they saw it; an oval enclosure with three entrances surrounded by a deep fosse full of scrub-oaks, a high vallum and another rampart like a ring around the whole. A prehistoric burial mound bulges under the heather inside one of the entrances.

The tragic tale of John Walford the Over Stowey charcoal-burner that Poole related to them one day in 1798, when they passed the rotting post of the nine-year-old gibbet, haunted both Wordsworth and Coleridge who both mistakenly recollected his name as Robert. He was born in 1765, a contemporary of Poole who remembered him plainly as he did Ann Rice, the miller's daughter—did she continue to live in Over Stowey?—and the half-witted Jane Shorney they forced Walford to marry by licence in Over Stowey church on 4 June 1789 and who was probably related to the Shorneys at the Castle of Comfort Inn where she wanted to go to drink cider on her last night, 5 July 1789. After execution on 20 August, Walford's body was cut down, put in an iron frame or cage and drawn up on the 30-foot gibbet to hang facing the cottage of his parents. For a year it hung, a blood-chilling sight to all who passed, especially to his old acquaintances, and then, after continual swinging and turning, it fell to the ground and was buried 'by common consent' of men in the neighbourhood ten foot deep beneath the gibbet. Wordsworth describes a similar hideous execution and its aftermath at the end of his 'Salisbury Plain', the long poem where he thought of introducing a character called Robert Walford. What he did instead was to embark on writing a long poem called 'A Somersetshire Tragdy' that told the tale of Walford and his love for the miller's daughter Ann Rice—called Agnes in the poem—who came forward to kneel in the executioner's cart with her lover. Eventually he left the unfinished poem with Poole. At Poole's death the Rev William Nichols, author of *The Quantocks and their Associations*, bought the MS from John Evered Poole and sold it to Gordon Wordsworth who, apparently, thought either that the theme was too sordid or the poem too unworthy and cut its pages out of Wordsworth's notebook.

In 1969 Radio 3 broadcast an opera *The Charcoal Burner* based on Walford's story. Thomas Wilson composed the music, Edwin Morgan wrote the libretto.

Coleridge wrote all his greatest poetry when he lived in Somerset, Wordsworth produced his afterwards, yet where the influence of the Somerset environment is integral to the poetry Wordsworth wrote in 1798, in Coleridge's poems it is mainly incidental, apart from poems written at Clevedon and such scenic poems as 'To a Beautiful Spring in a Village', 'Brockley Coombe', 'Shurton Bars'. It is none the less interesting to trace the signs of local influence especially as reading Coleridge's poems with this in mind makes plain that he and Dorothy looked at many things not only together but sometimes with the same eyes.

In 'The Foster Mother's Tale' written between March and June 1797 a little influence of his walks round Adscombe and neighbouring Friarn seems apparent. Certainly he had found the monks' ruined chapel and learned that land at Friarn formerly belonged to the friars of Bridgwater, just as he noticed the mosses and the brambles tufted with sheep's wool. The poem 'Love' reveals that he had walked the lonely road leading from Park End over the flank of Bagborough Hill and passing the gate of Cothelstone park which at that date made part of an estate called Tirhill. The ruined tower 'wild and hoary', 'half-way up the mount' was the folly or square tower of red sandstone that still stands on the park-slope, half-hidden by brambles and in a state of greater ruin. The maiden Genevieve 'leaned against the armèd man, The statue of the armèd knight', and here he stands, 'a grey stone rudely carved' as Coleridge's first draft said, the crude, upright, heavy figure of a man—mutilated by modern hooligans—naked except for his flung-back cloak although people remember his wearing a breast-plate fastened on with a wooden peg. The hole for the peg is visible, and another in his right hand shows where he held sword or spear. He has a dog at his feet.

This statue is marked on the 6in ordnance map.

The Stowey period, if one discounts his heavy financial worries, was the halcyon time of Coleridge's life, looked at in retrospect with yearning and something like incredulity.

Life went a-maying
With Nature, Hope and Poesy,
When I was young!

he wrote in 1823, adding to his poem a note in prose revealing that the memory of that youthful heyday identified itself with a certain early-summer morning when, just before dawn, he was walking over the Quantocks and stopped to listen to a nightingale in a copse at the very moment the first skylark soared from a green cornfield, sending down 'a song-fountain'. Almost idyllic days at Stowey—at a date before he knew the Wordsworths— reflect themselves in his poem to his disapproving brother, the Rev George Coleridge. In this he mentions not only hours of content over 'a social bowl' by the hearth of the Lime Street cottage while the winter wind shrilled at his window and rattled the frame, but delicious May evenings when, presumably with Sara, he sat in his orchard on the ancient apple-tree that was 'crooked earthward' but nevertheless made a roof of bloom over their heads on which the petals dropped. This was the tree Poole took grown-up Hartley to see, and a vision of the same old tree rises in that lovely meditative poem 'Frost at Midnight', written in February 1798 while Stowey slept under glimmering roofs, but in this poem the tree has snow on its branches and a perched robin singing so that it brings to mind Dorothy Wordsworth's February picture of snowy trees and a redbreast.

Another of the great reflective poems (his Conversation poems) written at Stowey is 'Fears in Solitude (written in April 1798 during the Alarm of an Invasion)'. The poet lies in a green combe between hills that flaunt golden patches of flowering furze, and while the skylark sings he endures his own agonised meditation on war, suffering, the horrors of invasion, treachery. Evening comes, bringing a sense of peace as dew draws out the scent of furze. The declining sun sends a beam to slant across the 'ivied beacon' on the summit, a reminiscence, perhaps, of the round tower or folly on Cothelstone Hill that is now a heap of ruins. (Cothelstone Hill is often called Cothelstone Beacon.) Coleridge climbs a green sheep-track to view from the hilltop a huge panorama magnificently framed in the poem: the dim sea, the broad fields shaded by many elms, the tower of Stowey church, the 'four huge elms' marking out Tom Poole's house that hid the Lime Street cottage. Coleridge still spoke of 'belovèd Stowey' when he wrote 'Fears in Solitude'. Actually the Quantock scene in it is, in part, a composite one since his own note tells us that he wrote the poem on 'the hill above Stowey' which would be the Mount at the top of Castle Hill, the furzey site of Nether Stowey castle of which the motte is still visible. This vantage-point would give him the wide view he pictured, but no combe lies very near Castle Mount.

He again mentioned Tom Poole's elms, enveloped in ivy, in 'This Lime Tree Bower My Prison' that he wrote that June day in Tom Poole's lime-shaded arbour, as well as Poole's walnut tree and the beautiful lime itself with leaves transparent in sunlight —vanished trees now. But his friends walking the Quantocks saw another splendid prospect that he painted: hilly fields, meadows, many steeples, and the sea where a sailing-ship glided between Steep Holm and Flat Holm, purple islands in the sunset. In the earlier part of the poem and earlier in the day, Coleridge conjured up the clearest picture ever made of the other place where his friends lingered: the glen at Alfoxden, 'the roaring dell'. The narrow combe, the noisy waterfall, the woods speckled with sun, the stream bridged by the fallen ash with its pallid leaves, the dank ferns and dark green water-weeds hanging from the wet stones on the edge of the waterfall—all are there.

The Alfoxden ambience is noticeable in 'The Three Graves' that Coleridge wrote mainly at Alfoxden after Wordsworth had written part of it. The woody dell within sound of the church bell, its brook with a bed of moss at the side, it is Holford Glen again, not far from Holford church and away from pastures, as the poem says. The hollies that made a round arbour hung with berries, not far from the brook, are the hollies of Alfoxden. They even appear again in 1801 in Coleridge's little fragment 'An Angel Visitant' where the holly twined with woodbine might even be the same tree as the one Dorothy, obviously with Coleridge's poetry in her head, described in a letter to Lady Beaumont in 1806:

'I never saw so beautiful a shrub as one tall holly which we had near a house we occupied in Somersetshire. It was attired with woodbine, and upon the very top of the topmost bough that "looked out at the sky" was one large honeysuckle flower like a star crowning the whole'.

'The Nightingale' is, of all Coleridge's poems, the poem peculiarly Dorothy's. He wrote it during that month of April when he walked with her so often, although her journal records that she walked to Stowey with him on the Sunday night of 6 May, 'heard the nightingale, saw a glow-worm'. Nightingales can be heard singing in several wooded places in the Quantocks during April and May, although their number has lessened, and until recently a glow-worm on a bank was not a rarity. The place where Dorothy and Coleridge listened to the 'love-chant' of the nightingales and saw them perched on twigs, was almost certainly Holford Glen, (seemingly mentioned again with its brook and couch of moss). The unnamed listeners 'rest on this old mossy bridge', 'see the glimmer of the stream'; a little later, Coleridge apostrophises 'my friend, and my friend's sister!' It is not likely that the 'gentle maid' who glided along pathways and knew all the nightingale-notes was Ellen or Mary Cruickshank as some have suggested, or any one else but Dorothy, who had shared the night-walks of Coleridge's most memorable spring.

Again here is a poem whose Quantock elements combine to make a picture that no one could consider topographically precise. The 'castle huge which the great lord inhabits not' is certainly not Alfoxden. Enmore Castle was the only huge castle in the neighbourhood. Contemporary drawings show an enormous building, turreted and moated, an eighteenth-century fake of a medieval stronghold situated in wooded countryside where nightingales still sing. If Coleridge had Enmore Castle in mind, he *did* mean Ellen Cruickshank or her sister Mary when he wrote of the gentle maid 'who dwelleth in her hospitable home Hard by the Castle', yet the 'Lady vowed and dedicate To something more than Nature' irresistibly suggests Dorothy Wordsworth. Moreover Enmore Castle was not uninhabited by its owner nor—as the poem describes—surrounded by wild neglected groves with tangled underwood and by 'once-trim walks' overgrown with grass and kingcups. If not entirely imaginary this description might apply to the deserted site of Nether Stowey Castle or to that of Stogursey Castle ruins (still in evidence) that Coleridge had seen when visiting the Pooles at Shurton Court.

It is in the 'Ancient Mariner' and in Part I of 'Christabel', that magical poem he was working on during the first three months of 1798, that affinity with Dorothy's journal is most apparent, revealing how closely these two minds were attuned. Sometimes Coleridge used one of Dorothy's entries. The broad-breasted oak, green with moss, is Dorothy's old Alfoxden oak on its turf-platform with 'its crooked arm pointing upward', and the last red leaf on a topmost twig is the solitary leaf Dorothy compared to a rag blowing in the March wind. Her entry on 24 March commenting on the tardy arrival of spring gave rise to Coleridge's line about spring's slow coming, and in the same stanza he creates a night-sky where thin cloud dulls and diminishes a full moon. This makes a striking parallel with Dorothy's observation of the sky on the wet night she and William came past the Castle of Comfort when cloud came over a 'moon immensely large . . . contracting the dimensions of the moon'.

The crying of the owls, the howling of the mastiff, are sounds that Dorothy recorded hearing on winter nights.

As for the carvings in Christabel's chamber, rich and strange fantasies wrought 'out of the carver's brain', they suggest that Coleridge saw the wealth of Tudor carvings, some of them fantastic and grotesque, in the churches of Stogursey and Crowcombe, Broomfield and Spaxton.

During the November walk to Watchet, the haunting story of the Ancient Mariner began shaping itself, if nebulously, in Coleridge's mind. Its scope soon outgrew that of the originally intended ballad that might sell for £5. On and off, for three months, Coleridge worked at it, temporarily laying 'Christabel' aside, and on 23 March 1798 the Wordsworths were the first people to hear those charmed and evocative stanzas that have enchanted so many at the first hearing. The pattern of the poem is interwoven with allusions that have their counterpart in Dorothy's journal: the hidden brook singing quietly all night to the leafy woods; the ivy-tod heavy with snow; the whooping owlet; the hermit's rotted oak-stump plumply cushioned with moss like those in Alfoxden park; the brown skeletons of leaves beside a brook that are the old, sere leaves Dorothy noticed the oaks and beeches retained in February; the 'restless gossamers, to which the thin sails of the phantom ship are compared, that are the 'restless spiders' threads' Dorothy saw quivering on the grass of the Quantock heath.

The little harbour, the kirk on the hill above it, have often been identified with Watchet harbour and the distant church of St Decuman. If Coleridge had a Somerset original in mind, he was just as likely to be remembering Clevedon when he composed his lines about 'the harbour-bay as clear as glass'. The harbour, the bay, the rocks and his description of a kirk standing very high above the rock, absolutely fits Clevedon's old parish church of St Andrew that was always a sea-mark, visible to ships in the bay as it stands almost on the edge of the cliff-top. It is likely that each of these harbours had a lighthouse. Topographical writers state that pastures and cornfields ran down to the sea at Clevedon before the carriage-road was made to connect the town and the ancient church, so that it is possible that a wood 'sloped down to the sea' as in the 'Ancient Mariner'.

As for walks, the few pages of the *Alfoxden Journal* make it plain that the Wordsworths and Coleridge must have familiarised themselves with all the paths and tracks over the Quantock hills as well as with the prehistoric trackway that runs along the ridge and with the so-called Great Road that runs from the dog pound up to, and alongside, the row of twisted and half-dying beeches on Longstone Hill overlooking Alfoxden. Of course they frequently used the main road (A39) from Holford to Stowey passing the Castle of Comfort Inn and the park of Woodlands where Poole's friend Willmott lived at the farmhouse. (They often took a field-path to Woodlands.)

In addition they knew the two main roads which carts and carriages used for crossing over the Quantocks, that are still called by the names then in use; the Stowey Road (a very ancient name) that, after Castle Hill in Nether Stowey runs from Bincombe Green over the hills to join the old Coach Road—the other road they knew—on the top at Dead Woman's Ditch

whence it continues past Crowcombe Park Gate before sending
off a branch-road that drops steeply to Crowcombe. The downward path of this road lies in a deep and beautiful combe over-
arched by splendid trees (lately, many have been felled). When
Dorothy wrote of using 'the Crookham way' she may have meant
the Coach Road which starts by the Counting House, not far from
the Castle of Comfort and which is sign-posted 'Crowcombe 3
miles'. This road which is still winding, solitary, tree-shaded, wet
with streams, runs above Five Lords Combe, where traces of
charcoal-pits can be found and where the deer sometimes feed in
winter among the scrub-oaks, then along the side of Great Bear.
It led the Wordsworths past the bare tortured thorn-tree of
Wordsworth's poem leaning askew somewhere on the summit
among heather, whortleberry and bracken.

When Dorothy and Coleridge went with William to Crowcombe one day in April and left him 'to make the appeal' they
themselves parted 'at the top of the hill' according to her account,
which means that they walked back up the steep road in the ferny
combe from Crowcombe and parted near Dead Woman's Ditch
—which, incidentally, is not connected with the Walford murder
as has been sometimes stated. From here Coleridge went home
to Stowey via the Stowey Road and Dorothy to Holford via the
Coach Road unless she took the brown path over Hare Knap.
Less than a fortnight later she walked again to Crowcombe—she
does not say whether William went—where she roamed the
grounds of Crowcombe Court, the handsome manor-house of red
brick and golden Ham stone built in 1725 that has been extens-
ively damaged by fire and wears a forlorn appearance greatly
regretted by those who remember its former distinguished looks.
Dorothy Wordsworth deplored the fact that the owners had
'deformed' the park and grounds by adorning them according to
eighteenth-century fashion with artificial ruins and hermitages.
The grounds still hold the broken arches of Cardinal Beaufort's
chapel which is a genuinely ancient chapel transplanted from
Halsway Manor (just off the Taunton—Minehead road).

Dorothy pronounced the 'dell', by which she always meant
combe or valley, as 'romantic and beautiful, though everywhere
planted with unnaturalised trees' which implies that she looked

with a critical eye at the trees planted on each side of the steep ascent from Crowcombe to the Quantocks and found them in some way unsuited to the landscape. Thomas Carew planted the woods when he built the court ninety years before her visit. What would she think of the modern conifer forests in the Quantocks?

With the two men Dorothy sometimes climbed the hill dividing the two combes at Holford. They must have taken the rough path that today branches left of the Bowling Green (at that time the common and without houses) to lead up to the slopes of Hare Knap. The combes are Holford Combe, indicated by the left arm of the signpost near the church and in which most of the village is built, and Hodder's Combe opening onto the common. (The name Holford Combe often gets transferred). Dorothy distinguished them as 'the lesser combe' and 'the greater combe' when she did not simply write 'in the evening up the combe' or 'fetched eggs from the combe'. Many a time she walked up Holford Combe, past Combe House (now a hotel) into Butterfly Combe—to which, later, the cottage of the tanner and his big mill-wheel now standing idle by Combe House gave the name Tannery Combe—where the stream, overlooked by Danesborough on her left, ran out of an over-branched pool where the deer drank at night. At least twice she followed the stream past the pool, using stepping-stones set in places where the path changes sides, finding the ground very soggy as she skirted Butterfly Wood and Swinage Wood, until she triumphantly found, near Lady's Wood, the little silver spring that is the stream's source, welling out of the hillside. It bears the centuries-old name of Lady's Fountain. After that she swung to her right to make a wide arc 'home over hilltops' and came down onto the common at Holford.

Sometimes the Wordsworths went with Coleridge or little Basil to Kilve, by way of Pardlestone Lane—a long walk for a young child—passing the Alfoxden Farm Bartholomew occupied. At Putsham they followed the lane, opposite the house called Kilve Court (now a college), past Kilve Mill, worked by the Holford stream on the last lap of its journey, past Kilve church to Priory Farm where, in the field hollowed by empty fish-ponds they saw the ruins of Kilve Chantry, erroneously called Kilve Priory, that had not then been gutted by the fire caused by nineteenth-century smugglers. Beyond the fields lay the sea, and perhaps William created suspicion by looking out through the pocket-telescope he possessed. On a rainy day they sheltered under fir-trees at Putsham, the main part of Kilve parish. Dorothy admired the flowery cottage gardens at Kilve and would still remember them when touring Scotland.

The small seaport and market-town of Watchet lay inside the parish of St Decumans that included four hamlets and the village of Williton now grown into a little town. The parish got its name from the fine hilltop church of St Decuman, a Celtic saint, that dominates town and harbour so commandingly that it is quite reasonable to identify it as the 'kirk' of the 'Ancient Mariner'. The total population of St Decumans was 1,600. Coleridge and the Wordsworths, as we know, approached Watchet in the gathering dark of a November day after walking over the hills to St Audries (then West Quantoxhead) and taking the righthand road (unnumbered) past the present St Audries Garage to descend to Watchet via Doniford. A lonely road then, where today we see caravans, chalets, an army camp: fields on each side, rooks flying homeward, gulls crying, the Quantocks behind, and ahead the dull sheen of the Bristol Channel with a few lights down below in the dusky town and round the harbour. An acrid smell hung in the damp air, caused by burning the seaweed called 'oare' that grew along the coast near Watchet. Burning it produced kelp that was exported for use in the manufacture of coarse glass bottles.

Walking the ribbed brown sands that grey morning the three friends saw sloops and smacks that perhaps included the *Sociable Friends* and the *Royal Charlotte* tied-up in a prettier harbour than we see today, for its waters were clearer and cleaner and so were those of the Watchet stream that impetuously empties into it. Since the rebuilding of the badly damaged harbour in 1900 the water at low tide is very muddy.

By 1797 Watchet's trade had sadly declined. Kelp was now the chief export. Other exports were limestone and the local alabaster used for making monuments. Like Defoe and Collinson, the Wordsworths and Coleridge saw the striking range of cliffs stretching along the Watchet coast, all streaked with various colours by their veins of blue lias, red sandstone and gypsum, and containing many fossils and 'walls' of alabaster. The herring fishery too had declined, but at low tide fishermen still set their nets on stakes at the far edge of the shore.

Viewing Watchet from the seaward side, one sees some very old overhanging houses with oriel windows and one with diagonal timbering that the travellers saw in 1797 as well as the London Inn where perhaps they slept. The view of St Decuman's Church from the sea was less obstructed than now.

In a note made years later Wordsworth stated that they went on from Watchet to Dulverton and came back the same way. Neither he nor Dorothy gave any details. One conjectures that they took the obvious route through Dunster (A396 turning left off A39) then southward up through the very beautiful valley of the river Avill with its wealth of trees whose autumn colours they were too late to see. In November when the coach-loads of sightseers no longer crowd the streets, Dunster looks much as they saw it in 1797. As they entered they saw the folly-tower on Conygar Hill, only twenty years old, then the Luttrell Arms Inn and the long street of Tudor houses with its octagonal Yarn Market all dominated by Dunster Castle crowning the hill at the far end. Near the Castle approach they turned right and walked past the beautiful church that hides the priory dove-cote and barn.

Their route took them up a steep climb along the south bank of the Avill through the village of Timberscombe and on to Cutcombe where Sir Philip Hales of Cannington owned a lot of land and where the people were very poor and 'like slaves to their superiors'. They saw a splendid sweep of the Brendon Hills as they walked this road towards Wheddon Cross with rolling Exmoor ahead of them and a stronger wind buffeting their bodies. From Wheddon Cross they walked alongside tumbling Quarme Water until it met the Exe, then nine miles of road through the lovely Exe valley until they came to the stone bridge called Hele Bridge a mile from their journey's end. From Dunster to Dulverton they covered fourteen miles of turnpike road, diverging no doubt to take a field-path whenever a local inhabitant indicated a short-cut.

It is regrettable that no written matter, whether prose or poetry, exists to give their impressions of the strange wild country they had traversed, nor of the little market-town Dulverton where they stayed a night and where they roamed round next morning and looked on the Exmoor-born river Barle rushing bright and shallow over its rocky bed. During the expedition they must have seen horned Exmoor sheep, cattle, wild colts, blackcock, sometimes a planing buzzard, trout in the rivers and their tributary streams with stone-chats and wagtails on the wet stones, and, if they were lucky, herons, a kingfisher or even an otter.

At the beginning of November the trio had done the long walk that became a favourite one, Porlock—Lynton, after continuing along the present A39 from Minehead. They stayed a night in Porlock, possibly at the Ship Inn where Southey stayed in 1799. The Porlock—Culbone part of the walk had been done by Coleridge earlier in the autumn when he wrote 'Kubla Khan', unless one accepts the theory still held by many Coleridge readers that he turned aside from the walk now described because he was ill with dysentery.

Nowadays Porlock devotes itself for nearly half the year to the tourist industry so that the narrow streets teem with cars and pedestrians. Divest it in imagination of its car-parks, souvenir shops and villas, and you may still see much of the little town of 600 inhabitants the Wordsworths and Coleridge knew in 1797. The small fifteenth-century manor-house called Doverhay, the church of St Dubricius with its spire truncated by a storm early in the eighteenth century, the white cottages overhung with thatch and garlanded with climbing roses, the harbour full of boats that today are pleasure-craft instead of the fishing-boats and cargo boats bringing in coal and lime. (There is a former Lime Path at Porlock Weir.) Collinson wrote a clear description in 1791:

> The situation of the town is finely romantick being nearly surrounded, on all sides, except towards the sea, by steep and lofty hills intersected by deep vales and hollow glens. The vallies between these hills are very deep and picturesque, the sides being steep, scarred with wild rocks and patched with woods. Most of the roads and fields are so steep that no car-

riages of any kind can be used: all the crops are, therefore, carried in with crooks on horses.

The main road to Lynton, the present A39, mounted the immensely steep and hazardous Porlock Hill that in later years the mail-coach horses, six at a time, and motor-cars too in their turn would find almost insurmountable. Those who shun it today take the Toll Road, starting near the Ship. Years after the Wordsworths' visits, this road with its easier gradients, its superb wooded surroundings, its glimpses of Porlock Bay, was cut through Mr Blathwayt's grounds. It joins the A39 at the top on Porlock Common where the traveller stands to look out on an open prospect of sea bounded only by the coast of Wales or southward to an equally unobstructed view of Exmoor's seemingly limitless hills and deeply-cut combes. To reach Lynmouth and finally Lynton, the goal of Coleridge and his friends, he must follow A39 down steep Countisbury Hill, in all a distance of about twelve miles from Porlock.

The Wordsworths and Coleridge took this steeply descending hill-road down into Lynmouth, but they did not have the Toll Road as their alternative to Porlock Hill. They took the coastal path starting at Porlock Weir and going up through Culbone: a longer way, solitary, secluded and hard going.

'Our road lay through woods rising almost perpendicularly from the sea,' wrote Dorothy, and Coleridge called them 'the hanging woods'.

The road they followed starts behind the Anchor Inn and leads past the lodge of the Italianate house Ashley Combe built by the Lovelaces in the mid-nineteenth century for Byron's daughter, its first mistress. The road becomes a track (with a right of way) climbing stiffly through mixed woods of oak, fir, larch, chestnut, planted on cliff-terraces so that every small gap frames a vignette of bluish-silver sea, of rocks, or of a boat. At intervals Wordsworth, Dorothy and Coleridge looked out on these as they climbed the steep-sided ravine which in November was sunless all day. They walked through wilder, stranger woods than those of today, woods haunted by more deer, foxes and badgers as well as by wild cats, to diminutive Culbone church

lying in the narrow dark ravine surrounded by an amphitheatre
of hills 1,200 feet high.

After that, did they take the wooded coastal path to wild and
beautiful Glenthorne (Devon) that today is overgrown with a
tangle of briers and bushes and is difficult to find and follow? If
so, they had to strike off from Glenthorne towards County Gate
(the Somerset—Devon boundary) and pick up the main Porlock—
Lynton road (our A39) that came over Culbone Hill and made
for the Countisbury descent. Since day was declining—they
reached Lynmouth at dusk—it seems more likely that from
Culbone they struck across the hilltop towards the main Porlock—
Lynton road.

Coleridge crossed the fields from Culbone to reach Ash Farm
(in Porlock parish) at whatever date he came. Today a very small
sign on the right of the A39 where, after Porlock Hill, this road
runs along the top, indicates: 'Culbone 2½ miles. Yearnor Farm
Bed & Breakfast'. Ash Farm can be reached by turning off here
through the left division of the white gate set over a cattle grid
and following a road across a plateau where scrub-pines hang
over the whortleberry, heather and fern.

Ash Farm, Yearnor, Broomstreet, Silcombe—each is a group
of grey stone buildings sheltering in a hollow of the wild moor.
Further on this road forks to make two rougher, narrower roads
of which one leads to Silcombe and the other—a moss-grown
lane—to Ash Farm, where in autumn the high cornfield still holds
corn-stooks, not bales. The farmhouse gives the impression of
age and sturdiness and cannot have changed its appearance much
since Coleridge knocked at the door at the side of the house,
although a newer porch shelters the door from wind and a
bullock-shippen joined to the end of the house has been trans-
formed into a pleasant room with oak beams. The age of the
house is demonstrated by the great long stone barn built on
to it as an integral part and by a tiny cobbled entry court
in front of a door near the bulging disused bread-oven on the
far side of the house. Here Coleridge could see the sea sleeping
in the moonlight—as he wrote—if he looked from a jutting bedroom window. He could not see it as he sat in the kitchen or
parlour where in any case he was lost in his opium-dream until

the 'person from Porlock' rode his horse into the yard at the top of the lane.

When Dorothy Wordsworth invited friends for a stay at Alfoxden she advised them to use the ferry below Bridgwater which would reduce their Bristol—Holford journey to thirty-six miles, according to her reckoning. De Quincey used it and so did Coleridge, following a path across the grazing-lands behind Pawlett Church to the Passage House.

The remaining fragments of the White House Inn represent the Passage House by the ferry and old people remember that at low tide—for the Parret is a tidal river—Combwich children sometimes ran across an old causeway made of blue lias stone to pick apples and blackberries from its abandoned orchard. They tell also that cattle and sheep could be driven across this river passage and that 'old squire' from Hill House told them he had ridden over when following the hounds. For years now the thick mud characteristic of the river Parret has buried the causeway, and the river-passage is only a memory. Yet the quaint off-the-map village that Combwich used to be before it became a harbour for the use of the nuclear power station at Hinkley Point is clearly remembered by many people; the village had much character although it was never beautiful. Its cottages were built mainly of the red brick once manufactured there and flat-bottomed boats lay in the creek. Coleridge on holiday once wrote that he might 'dart into Wales' and return by boat to Combwich.

Tom Poole obtained from Combwich the salmon he sometimes sent to his friends. He rode over to Combwich from Stowey (generally reached today by way of the road to Hinkley Point off the A39 at Cannington) and liked riding alongside the sluggishly flowing Parret that hardly ruffled itself until the bore surged in from the estuary and rolled up towards Bridgwater. Tom Poole enjoyed the lazy silence that sometimes enveloped the place on a still autumn day. On such a day he wrote to Coleridge who had walked or ridden there beside him and who, had Poole known it, had just left his Somerset haunts for the very last time, just after the long summer visit of 1807. Poole's description of Combwich is like a painting of the place on that cloud-veiled, warm September noon when, he said, not a leaf stirred, the lazy tide glided between sandbanks, a fisherman lay stretched out asleep in his boat with two rods and lines awaiting the fish, and the tops of vessels rose with roof-tops behind the trees, 'so tranquil, asleep yet awake'.

He rode back to Stowey from which his friends had departed.

Appendix

LATER HISTORY OF COLERIDGE'S COTTAGE

Various tenants, including the minister of the Congregational Chapel opposite (built in 1802) occupied Coleridge's former home in Lime Street until the middle of the nineteenth century. It then became the Coleridge Cottage Inn with the inn-sign hanging where the replica of Coleridge's portrait by Northcote now hangs. Thanks to the energetic efforts of the Rev William Greswell, rector of Dodington, near Nether Stowey, an appeal for funds was launched in October 1892, the 120th anniversary of Coleridge's birthday, so that the cottage might not fall into oblivion or ruin, and on 9 June 1893 a tablet made of stone from a Spaxton quarry was affixed to a wall, commemorating the fact that Coleridge had lived there. The ceremony of fixing the mural stone was fully described by Mr Greswell in the *Athenaeum* 17 June 1893. It had been attended by Dykes Campbell, Coleridge's editor and biographer, and by Coleridge's descendant and editor of his poems Ernest Hartley Coleridge who read a paper on Coleridge's life and work in Stowey. An appeal was launched for funds to lease the cottage for £15 a year with the aim of making the cottage 'a Coleridge reading-room or library'. A committee was formed with the Rev W. Greswell as treasurer.

In June 1908 Princess Louise, Duchess of Argyll, attended a meeting at Kensington Palace in support of a national appeal for funds. Lord Lytton took the chair and the people present included Lord Coleridge, Andrew Lang and Ernest Hartley Coleridge. Professor Knight, the Wordsworth scholar, who had done a great deal to raise funds, was absent through illness. By August 1908 the cottage had been bought and Mr Greswell appealed for 'relics, books, mementoes of the Nether Stowey set' to be contributed by any who owned them so that they might be stored in a room at the cottage (see *Bridgwater Mercury* 5 August 1908). In autumn 1909 the property was handed over to the National Trust.

NOTES

Three dates have been suggested for the writing of 'Kubla Khan' :
1) Early autumn 1797, as in this book
2) Late November 1797
3) Spring 1798

Several Exmoor farms have been suggested as the place where 'Kubla Khan' was written. Broomstreet Farm is a possible alternative to Ash Farm. Coleridge, in a note written years later, said that the farm lay ¼ mile from Culbone church. This marks Ash Farm as a more likely place than Broomstreet.

The older name Alfoxden has been used in this book. Coleridge and the Wordsworths always used it, with variations of spelling. For some years now the house has been called Alfoxton Park.

None of the Somerset houses associated with Coleridge and Wordsworth is open to the public except Coleridge's cottage at Nether Stowey (National Trust).

Alfoxton Park is a hotel. There is a right-of-way through the park.

The statue of the armed knight referred to in Coleridge's poem 'Love' is much more likely to have been the statue at Tirhill in the Quantocks than the recumbent effigy in Sockburn church which has been suggested.

BIBLIOGRAPHY

Ashton, H. *William & Dorothy* (1938)

Atthill, Robin *Old Mendip* (Newton Abbot 1964)

Bateson, F. W. *Wordsworth: a re-Interpretation* (1954)

Beer, J. B. *Coleridge the Visionary* (1959)

Billingsley, J. *General View of the Agriculture of the County of Somerset* (1798)

Blunden, E. & Griggs, E. L. *Studies of Coleridge by several hands* (1934)

Carpenter, M. *The Indifferent Horseman* (1954)

Chambers, E. K. *A Sheaf of Studies* (1942)

Chambers, E. K. *S. T. Coleridge: a Biographical Study* (1938)

Coburn, K. *Inquiring Spirit* (1951)

Coburn, K. *The Notebooks of S. T. Coleridge, Vol. I* (1957)

Coleridge, E. H. (ed). *Poems of S. T. Coleridge* (1921)

Collinson, J. *History of Somerset* (1791)

Cottle, J. *Early Recollections of Coleridge & Southey* (1837)

Crosse, C. *Red Letter Days* (1892)

Darbishire, H. (ed). *Journal of Dorothy Wordsworth* (1958)

Darbishire, H. *The Poet Wordsworth* (1950)

Dilks, T. B. *Charles James Fox & the Borough of Bridgwater* (Bridgwater 1953)

Elwin, M. *The First Romantics*

Farr, G. *Somerset Harbours* (1954)

Greenwood. *Somerset Delineated* (1821)

Greswell, W. *The Land of Quantock* (Taunton 1903)

Griggs, E. L. *S. T. Coleridge: Collected Letters* (1956)

Hanson, L. *S. T. Coleridge: The Early Years* (1939)

Hazlitt, W. *My First Acquaintance with Poets*
House, H. *Coleridge* (1968)
House, H. *Coleridge: the Clark Lectures* (1953)
Jarman, S. G. *History of Bridgwater* (1889)
Legouis, E. *The Early Life of William Wordsworth* (1921)
Litchfield, R. B. *Tom Wedgwood, the First Photographer* (1903)
Lowes, J. D. *The Road to Xanadu* (1927)
Margoliouth, H. M. *Wordsworth & Coleridge* (1953)
Meteyard, E. *A Group of Englishmen* (1871)
Moorman, M. *William Wordsworth* (1965)
Murch, J. *History of the Presbyterian & General Baptist Churches* (1835)
Nicholls, W. *The Quantocks & their Associations* (1891)
Page, J. L. *Exploration of Exmoor* (1893)
Potter, S. *Minnow among Tritons* (1934)
De Quincey, T. *Reminiscences of the Lake Poets* (1834)
Reed, M. *A Wordsworth Chronology* (1967)
Roper, D. (ed). *Wordsworth & Coleridge: Lyrical Ballads* (1968)
de Selincourt, E. (ed). *Poetical Works of Wordsworth* (1950)
de Selincourt, E. (revised Chester Shaver) *Early Letters of William & Dorothy Wordsworth* (1935, 1967)
Warner. *Walk through the Western Counties of England* (1800)
Waters, B. *Severn Tide* (1953)
Whalley, G. *Coleridge & Sara Hutchinson* (1955)

PERIODICALS ETC

British Directory (1792)

'Article on Richard Reynell' *Illustrated London* 1893)

Chubb, M.	'A Forbear & his Hobby'	*The Countryman* (Winter 1963, Spring 1964)
Morley, E. J.	'Coleridge in Germany'	*London Mercury* (1931) XXIII
Sypher, Professor	'Coleridge's Somerset'	*Philological Quarterly*

ACKNOWLEDGEMENTS

I should like to express my sincere gratitude to the Bridgwater Borough Library, the Somerset County Library, and the Somerset Record Office for their unfailing help and co-operation. Thanks are due also to Mr Peter Pagan of Bath City Libraries for information and to Bristol City Library for the use of material.

I am greatly indebted to the Rev E. Davies for detailed information about the Bridgwater and Taunton Unitarian chapels and for the use of their valuable documents, as well as to the Rev E. F. Awre of Nether Stowey and the Rev J. V. Bevan of Goathurst for allowing me to consult their church registers.

I am very grateful to Mr R. Clatworthy for showing me over Tom Poole's house in Castle Street, Nether Stowey and for supplying information about it; to Mrs Hart-Davis and Mrs Piper for showing me Poole's house in St Mary Street, Nether Stowey, to Mr A. J. Richards for allowing me to visit Ash Farm, Porlock, to Mr R. de Brugha for his information about Alfoxton House, and to Miss Mary Chubb and Mr John Chubb for kindly permitting reproduction of sketches by Coleridge's friend John Chubb. I gratefully acknowledge permission granted by the National Portrait Gallery to include the portrait of Coleridge and permission granted by the Somerset Archaeological Society to include the portrait of Wordsworth, and I wish to express sincere gratitude to Mr Hamilton Jenkin and Miss Ruth Phillips for valuable and documented information about the families Jenkin and Chester.

I regret the impossibility of viewing the interior of Coleridge's cottage at Clevedon.

INDEX